P| *tion*

Bad Education brings together and updates Phil Beadle's columns in *The Guardian* over the past six years. In them, he has brought a critical eye to bear on such topics as Michael Gove, OFSTED, the treatment of trans-gendered children, assessment for learning, ICT, the attack on political correctness and even chewing gum. His views are not always predictable – or entirely consistent – and the reader may be in for a few surprises. The book is in the best traditions of 'crap detection' and, even when you don't agree with Beadle, he makes y~

~ Emeritus,
of London

If like me, you hav~ ~joyed reading Phil Beadle's 'On Teaching' column in the *Education Guardian* over the years you will be delighted with this anthology ranging across Politics and Policy, Pedagogy, Performance, People and Personalities and Phil's great passion Literacy and English teaching. We have the authentic voice of this excellent classroom practitioner and education commentator who with wit and humour and penetrating insight provides an original, searching and provocative commentary into the educational changes over the last few years.

This book will entertain you but it will also make you think again about educational policy and practice.

Professor David Woods CBE, Chief Adviser for London Schools and Principal National Challenge Adviser

This is Phil Beadle at his feisty, acerbic best. He surveys the current educational landscape and leaves it scorched and smouldering, taking on attention-seeking politicians and madcap theorists and putting them firmly in their place. It's a book that's full of humour, provocation and plain unabashed common sense –

and which fights the all-important cause of good teachers and their pupils.

Bad Education is written with Beadle's trademark passion and exuberance. Time and again, he reminds us why we chose to become teachers, cutting through all the clutter and distractions that can mar our day-to-day work.

Keep a copy close at hand for the times when the world of education seems to have gone mad (which is rather too often these days): Beadle's book is like a thermos flask of reassurance and unpretentious wisdom. It's one of those texts we all need to sustain us through the tough times – a rare combination of a work that makes us feel better about ourselves whilst also challenging us to raise our game. It's the kind of book every teacher – and everyone who pontificates about teaching – needs to read.

Geoff Barton, Headteacher, King Edward VI School

Phil Beadle is a worthy successor to the late, great Ted Wragg as a chronicler of all that is best and worst in education and teaching. His 1000-word *Guardian* articles provide a dose of medicine that is guaranteed to alleviate the symptoms of teachers who look around them and find only contradictions. The articles are both amusing and deeply serious.

Phil Beadle's well-written, extremely readable articles challenge both orthodoxies and cant. They show the effects of the solutions in search of problems to which the education profession is constantly afflicted and they cry out for evidence-based policy to underpin the work of schools. Phil Beadle always imbues the latest crazy top-down policy with timeless bottom-up good sense and wit.

It is not only government ministers that come in for criticism, but also taxi drivers, quangocrats, editorial writers, academic selection, homophobia, ICT and much more.

A book to be read, dipped into and returned to again and again. But, above all, a book to be read by all who have the interests of young people and their teachers at heart.

John Dunford, Chair, Whole Education,
Chair, WorldWide Volunteering,
Chair, Chartered Institute of Educational Assessors

Has Phil Beadle been writing his column for *The Guardian* for only six years? It seems as if he's always been there, ready to comment on – or more likely drive a coach and horses through – the latest back-of-an-envelope government solution to the nation's educational deficiencies.

Here, just in case you missed any of them, or simply to recapture and dip into at leisure is a Beadle anthology. The pieces deal with just about all of the staffroom coffee-break, anger-management, you-couldn't-make-it-up issues that came up during the period covering the long twilight of New Labour and the dawn of the multi-coloured swapshop that is the Coalition.

Right at the outset he has the measure of what drives the Cameron–Gove approach to education. It's '… entirely concerned with lucre and its redistribution away from the pockets of schoolteachers.' This they will achieve, he explains, by sidelining local authorities and in the process diminishing the power of the teacher unions.

It's that straight cut to the chase that makes Beadle essential reading. His swipes are widely distributed. He's bothered at the way "teaching" is being pushed out by "learning", for example – '… whilst teaching will often cause learning, learning will only in very sad circumstances cause teaching.'

That doesn't mean he's always in favour of the way teachers work – or are persuaded to work. He has a go at the tyranny of the 'four-part lesson', and the writing of lesson objectives on the board.

Of course he can annoy us along the way – he shouldn't forget that it was the very ICT enthusiasts he has a pop at who were the first to cry out against the abuse of PowerPoint and interactive whiteboards. That, though, is part of the relationship between Beadle and his readers. He isn't handing out comfort blankets.

Part of that edginess is seen in some of the more serious and much needed challenges you'll find here. Every teacher knows, for example, that, in Beadle's words, 'British schools are the final, blithe bastions of homophobia, which is, and has always been, at epidemic proportions in them.' His use of 'blithe' here is appropriate because, he goes on, 'Homophobia, in British schools, is the last remaining acceptable prejudice.'

Every teacher needs to read this book. More importantly, every head teacher and governor needs to read it. And even more importantly still, every administrator and politician needs to read it too. And when they encounter, as some members of all those groups surely will, passages that make them throw the book across the room, let me appeal to them to pick it up and read that bit again, this time with a bit of thought and a lot of humility. Because they'll find that Beadle's great strength lies in the fact that behind the ire and the feisty polemic lies a lot of thought and humility of his own, and plenty of humanity too.

Gerald Haigh, former teacher,
head teacher, school governor and author

PHIL BEADLE

THE GUARDIAN COLUMNS
Foreword by Will Woodward, Head of Politics at the *Guardian*

Crown House Publishing Limited
www.crownhouse.co.uk
www.crownhousepublishing.com

First published by
Crown House Publishing Ltd
Crown Buildings, Bancyfelin, Carmarthen, Wales, SA33 5ND, UK
www.crownhouse.co.uk
and
Crown House Publishing Company LLC
6 Trowbridge Drive, Suite 5, Bethel, CT 06801, USA
www.crownhousepublishing.com

First published 2011.

British Library of Cataloguing-in-Publication Data. A catalogue entry
for this book is available from the British Library.

10-digit ISBN 184590683-7
13-digit ISBN 978-184590683-2

LCCN 2010937328

Printed and bound in the UK by
Gomer Press, Llandysul, Ceredigion

Acknowledgements

We are grateful to Guardian News and Media Ltd for permission to reproduce the material in this book.

Preface

In 2004 the then editor of *The Guardian*'s education supplement came to see me teach. We chatted briefly after the lesson, and for some reason I decided that it would be amusing to wind him up by pretending that I was married to Marian Bighead, then Deputy Editor of *The Times*. (I have never even been in the same room as her and, to date, have no explanation as to why I enjoy completely unnecessary lying so much.)

He recognised in me a flagrant lack of something, and a few months later asked me to write a public apology for my behaviour at an awards ceremony that he too had attended. This included the phrase 'significantly over-refreshed' and made reference to 'having cleverly slept in my suit'.

It is now 2011. My column entitled 'On Teaching' has run in *The Guardian*'s education pages for seven odd years. This book is an anthology of those columns.

Aside from being a husband and a father, it has been the defining honour of my existence having been gifted the permission to write about education for what I regard as the most politically important and vital organ in British life. And I extend my profound thanks to the editors who have guided me delicately through the process of sculpting readable copy: particularly Will Woodward, Claire Phipps and Alice Woolley, who, though I have never met her, is one of my favourite people.

Foreword

Phil Beadle has never impressed me as much as he did the first time I met him. He was in a classroom, teaching in one of the less fragrant parts of east London; and I was watching him, judging – the layperson in a trio deciding whether he should be named secondary schoolteacher of the year. His lesson was extraordinary – magnetic and dynamic, brimming full of ideas – transcending even the obvious but necessary artifice of the event (his students knowing that we were watching him) – risky and eyebleedingly fast-paced. I'd like to pretend, particularly to Phil, that I had swung it for him in a Twelve Angry Men sort of way. But it was, as they say, a unanimous verdict. My two colleagues, both wise, retired teachers, could see what I could fumble towards, that this guy could walk the walk and talk the talk. We had our winner.

Shortly after that he became famous.

And shortly after that he became one of our columnists.

The two events are connected, and not only because chippy, frustrated rock stars, who also used to work in the city and decide to become teachers and then become among the most gifted practitioners of their generation, do on the face of it at least have the potential to be pretty interesting to *Guardian* readers. I was editing *Education Guardian* and, with an eye on what could transpire, I asked him to write a piece about his award-winning night (he got drunk; he lost a laptop; he banged his head on the underside of a chair that he slept under. He'll tell you the rest). It was, not unlike his lessons, snappy and funny and true. Much to my delight he repeated a line he had used on me as he descended the stairs backstage at Drury Lane, clasping his Teaching Awards gong, which moderately appalled me at the time. The Poster Boy Of Inner City Education could write, too.

'On Teaching' (a Ronseal name for a column if ever there was one) was launched a few weeks later. I've moved jobs and no longer commission him and I read him as an interested amateur. I like the chalkface ones the best, the war stories from the classroom; and the elegant skewerings of the latest faddish piece of education theory or (often IT-related) me-tooism. Looking back over the seven years I'm struck by how optimistic some of the early ones feel, redolent of that mid-Blair era where the money was starting to stream into the empty reservoirs of school budgets and teachers' pockets, by how the kind of teacher that Phil represented was beginning to blossom in a more benign political climate, as if in some kind of post-revolutionary spring. It doesn't feel that way now.

After Ted Wragg died I hoped Phil could fill some of the crater-sized hole left by that giant of a writer, and Phil wrote even more regularly for us, in Ted's slot, more generalised comment pieces. Phil gave that up after a while, fearing it was too much and that the original column was suffering. He was probably right. Ted was – still is – irreplaceable; Phil was – is – his own man, too iconoclastic to be exactly the voice of teaching in the way Ted was. But I hope it doesn't besmirch either man to say that Phil's writing has some of the spirit of Ted's – generosity, a candidness, an eye for the ridiculous; and passion. And more prosaically, but for the paper's purposes absolutely necessarily, a crossover appeal, an ability to engage the general reader and the professional reader in subjects that one may know nothing about and the other may know pretty much everything about. For a section like *Education Guardian*, that quality is pure gold.

PREFACE

Right now I don't think there's anybody writing the kind of thing that Phil does as well as Phil does. Compared to Teacher of the Year it's not much of an award but if there was one going for the most consistently enjoyable education writer in the British Isles, I very much doubt there would be much of a shortlist.

Will Woodward

Contents

The Learning Environment

Life in a Glass Dungeon

Whoever designed the school I've just started working at has obviously been properly briefed on the full range of stereotypical judgements it is possible to make on the young people who go there. Anyone's first impression on entering the building is that it bears a startling resemblance to Alcatraz, the key function appears to be the lockdown. And then you enter the classroom.

The wall decoration *du jour* in my new classroom appears to be the unpainted breeze block. Initially, I'd thought, perhaps foolishly, that this was some post-modern nuance of architectural philosophy. 'Ah. Well noted, Mr Beadle. We keep the walls functional as an inverse correlative of the school's approach to learning and, indeed, to teaching – should it exist. The hue of the walls serves to minimise visual noise, and the exquisite sparseness means children can project their thoughts, hopes and aspirations onto the blank, grey canvas of the brick.'

No such cobblers, I'm afraid. The walls aren't painted because, if they were, the building would fall down. Given that it houses 1,200 students and there's quite a lot of glass, this would be considered a bad thing.

Speaking of glass, not since my days as a Penge window cleaner's assistant have I seen quite so much of it. The school is, for a limited period only, at the bottom of the league tables, and this, of course, inevitably affects admissions. Consequently, there are several boys and girls in attendance to whom Mr Naughty is not a stranger. Last year, so I am told, this fatal combination of naughty boy and glass palace combined, in startling symbiosis with the presence of small stones in the bits where trees are planted, to produce an array of aural shivering effects and a glazing bill in the region of £13,000 per month.

The building is shaped like a cheese wedge, meaning that classrooms at the front of it have sloping ceilings in the region of over 30 feet high on the right-hand side, 8 feet high on the left. Personally, this leads me to feel I'm teaching in an educational version of the crooked house amusements one might find in a post-communist, Hungarian fairground; though the kids tend not to notice. What they do notice though is that the rooms are unbearably hot in the summer, and that the only windows available for opening are narrow-eyed fellers whose bottoms are some 29 feet up in the air.

Teachers responding to a class's complaints of stuffiness must involve themselves in a ridiculous ballet, in which, with the aid of the school's single 30-foot long pole, they attempt to co-ordinate their hand movements to unhook the window latch at a distance of what must feel to them like several miles. So extreme is this distance, that the merest half-tremor of the little finger can cause the hook to miss the latch by an acutely embarrassing distance. Whole double lessons are wasted as male students collapse into torrents of uncontrollable hysterics while gamine, female teachers attempt vainly to open a window. 'Face it, miss,' the boys chortle joyously and rhythmically, 'You ain't got the control to get the pole in the hole.'

When the window is finally opened, after several lessons marked by much hilarity and little learning, no one notices the breeze, of course; it's 30 feet up! A whisper across the foothills of heaven. Of no use at all to the earthbound.

The second floor, however, is so well acquainted with the heavens it tempts students to pay an early visit to them. The main corridor is a balcony many miles above the ground, with only the frailest of railings separating students and teachers from a meeting with their maker. I have held informal chats with colleagues on that balcony, our backs glued with vertiginous fear to the wall furthest away from 'touching the void'.

'What do you think of so and so's attainment so far this year?'

'I don't know. I don't care about education. I'm going to fall. Fear the railing! Fear the railing!'

This would be bad enough were it not for the existence of the viewing platform. At one point the balcony sweeps out, in a grand arc, supported by nothing, leaving the foolhardy student or teacher who stands on it feeling exactly as safe and secure as if they were teetering at the edge of a promontory overlooking a Norwegian fjord, supported only by a thin elastic band.

Thankfully, no one has tipped over the edge just yet. The students seem to recognise some of the potential dangers the structure presents and behave appropriately on the top floor. And, in all honesty, this particular glass palace is a far better educational environment than, for instance, the school I worked in where there were so few tiles on the roof that a man (whom the kids had wittily named 'Rufus') had set up home there; or the school in which the toilets resembled the seventh circle of hell so accurately that you were given a special award for risking the hem of your trouser in the bosom of the sit-downs. (And at least no one thought it would be a sensible idea to put a trading floor in the atrium!)

So, yes, it is better to work in a glass palace than a decaying wreck. The students seem to feel that the building respects them, and behaviour and learning are both showing a marked up-turn. It wasn't like this last year, though, and the building was exactly the same. What reason then for the improvements? What reason for the fact that the glazing bill hasn't even reached £100 this month?

The reason is that a school is the human beings in it, not the fabric that surrounds them. The school in which I work is on a steep upward trajectory, and it is on this trajectory because the human beings in it, staff and students, are forcing it. It's all very well architects deciding to experiment on children with some of their more outré creative ideas, but if a school isn't managed well, it will fail, be it palace or dungeon.

Macramé versus Rio Ferdinand

You may find this column a bit listy. The reason you will find it so is that it is going to be written in list form: a list of all the display items found in the corridors of Rosebrook Community School in Mansfield, followed by the display items in a counterpoint secondary school. There is a point to this.

When you enter Rosebrook Community School, piped classical music (Vivaldi's *Four Seasons* as imagined by Nigel Kennedy) haunts and excites. You notice that behind your left shoulder there is a sound of trickling water, and turn to see a small indoor fountain laughing gaily, water gently tickling a bed of small stones. Following the direction of the sound, you come across a wall on which paper skeletons dance next to real X-rays of legs and diagrams of the human body: 'This is how we move and grow,' it says. On the opposite side of the entrance hall, slightly to your right, is a huge board covered in stars that have been cut out of Post-it notes and covered with glitter; on each star is the name of a child. There are hundreds of stars.

On entering the secondary school, you approach a reception desk over which is a sign bearing the school's name.

Past Rosebrook's central recess area, in which there are a few small chairs and a table for kids who need to just sit and chat, or for those odd occasions when they might need to talk with the head (you get a sense that they are deliberately that size so that in moments of crisis the head can sit and talk softly to his pupils, all the time aware that he will be able to empathise better with them if he somehow manages to get his robust frame on to the same level as their somewhat smaller bodies), there is a display of children's photos. These shining faces are accompanied by the kids' manifestos for election to the School Council; it seems every child in the school has been instilled with sufficient ambition to put themselves up for high office and, next to this, there is a wall display of work on Joseph's coat: kids have used ICT applications to design dreamcoats, constructed prototypes, made their own coats and then written evaluatory recounts in the form of acrostics, which are, of course, written on coat-shaped paper.

In the secondary school foyer/atrium there are some expensive windows and a poster of Rio Ferdinand pretending to read a book that is too hard for him.

The recess area at Rosebrook leads onto the main school corridor. Before you get to this though, you must pass the slideshow of lesson activities on a screen, the photos of kids' faces that have been warped, so that they resemble cartoon characters or Picasso pastels. On entering the corridor you are struck by the sheer craft involved; every single possible material is used to construct these displays: old newspaper is given fresh use, cut into the shapes of the leaves of palm trees, painted eggs hang from branches to form Easter Trees, year one's 'Man on the Moon Display' features tin foil, paper plates painted silver, and glitter everywhere; there are model spitfires, gas masks, Greek pots, fireworks, diaries, hot air balloons and tractors. Best of all, better than the rainforest the kids have constructed, better than the cocktail stick flags, the Medusa peg bags, better even than the detailed papier-mâché models of the water cycle, is the version of Monet's *Water Lilies* which covers a whole wall. This is so beautiful as to feel slightly out of context, hidden away in the far reaches of a corridor in a school at the edge of a Mansfield council estate. It is breathtaking! Using print, needlework, paint, threaded felt and shiny card, the children at Rosebrook have – together: collaboration towards a finished product is valued highly at the school – produced a work of art that, for me, shames the original.

Down the corridor in the secondary school Michael Owen is also pretending he enjoys reading. He has his thumbs up and a fake smile plastered across his gob.

Rosebrook Community School is a beautiful place for children to spend their time; a panoply of kaleidoscopic colour, an assault to the senses, a feast for eyes and brain. But these are not just pretty colours, visual noise to distract children from the drab nature of their work on the walls at Rosebrook. What the displays serve to show is the incredible palette of pedagogy on offer at the school. You get a sense that no lesson is ever wasted, no opportunity spurned. You get a sense of pride that you are involved in British education if you walk in there. I doubt that there isn't a school in the country that couldn't learn from it.

After three days at the school, I sit open mouthed in the head's office. 'Yes,' says the ball of energy and enthusiasm in front of me, 'The environment is important to our children. Our aim is to offer an education that's relevant and meaningful to them and that will prepare them for life beyond school. The world is full of colour and excitement and we try to recreate some of this in the environment in which they learn.'

The head of the secondary said, 'Yes, we've got a bit of work to do on display.'

Performance

Classroom Organisation

I shout at the television. I can't help it. The most recent recipient of my rage is *Location, Location, Location*. Not the programme itself. No, the bit that gets my goat, I mean really reduces me to a fit of purple-faced apoplexy, is where this week's identikit drab Northamptonian straights flounce into someone else's house and declare, 'Look at that space,' or 'Isn't the space glorious,' or 'I need some space (just temporarily mind).'

It is therefore with a meekness that would befit one about to inherit the largest of political concerns that I dip my toes into this very subject. Space: the forgotten frontier. The classroom tends not to be a resource we talk about very much, but the way you organise your desks says more about you than a performance development review ever can.

Broadly, there are three schools of thought on how you should organise desks in a classroom: the traditional, the progressive and the barmy. Traditional first: tables in rows or, more probably nowadays, in pairs. Eyes front. Look at the teacher. Sit up straight. Open your textbooks at page 34: do exercises 1 through to 12.

There is a place for this method of organisation. It is useful for tests and it is probably one of the safest ways of ensuring you have a class of compliant children who do not talk to each other.

But, if forcing children into straitjackets of compliance is what you entered the profession for, you are in the wrong job. There are logistical reasons, in certain curriculum areas, why desks have to be arranged in this way, but it always struck me as too Dickensian an approach. Tables in pairs, facing the front, call to mind images of lofty pedagogues waffling unintelligibly from on high about the school's three major educational priorities, 'Discipline! Discipline! Discipline!' As a strategy, it seems primarily motivated by fear of children and of their potential rebellion. It stops the young people in our care from talking to each other. And if you think a teacher is the sole vessel of knowledge and wisdom in a classroom you are ... well, you know.

Far better to take a step in the direction of the 'progressive'. It's a long held truism in education that, if you've got the guts, seating young people in groups profits both their education and their ability to perform basic social competencies. It encourages them to talk to each other. This is not something any teacher worth their shekel should fear. A classroom should be an intellectual environment. See your classroom as a cafe on the Left Bank, and your students as Parisian intellectuals in black roll-necks and berets. Allow them to discuss and investigate ideas. (Just be careful when handing out the Gauloises. This can be unpopular with the governing body.)

Children profit from investigative talk: they flourish in the realm of the 'idea'. It is better, really, that they undertake this journey together, without a captain at the table; that their epiphanies are not devalued by the close-up presence of someone who already seems to know everything.

So put your tables in groups, light the touchpaper and stand back. One quite reasonable objection might be that it denies the teacher a role in the centre of things; and, I admit, there are many of us who entered the classroom because the stage door was locked. There is a solution, however: the Comedy Club Classroom.

Have tables in five groups of six, and have them skewed at weird tangents and angles – this creates ambience. Ensure, however, that the tables are situated at the very ends of the room, near to the walls, leaving as big a central space as possible. Skewing the tables ensures that all the students on each desk can be focused on a central spot, which is, you guessed it, your – or their – performance space.

This way the teacher can choose. Your classroom is either the Parisian cafe where students talk over the idea you have given them to discuss, or you can be the egotist didact, imparting knowledge and effortlessly witty bons mots simultaneously.

There is also (so I have heard), a school of thought of one on this issue: the barmy. If we are to engage children, to retain their interest, to have them waiting in corridors excited at the prospect of every lesson we teach, then any set-up where we do the same thing every day should be anathema. Any seasoned expectation a pupil may have about what is – yawn – going to happen in our lessons should be liable to being shattered at any moment.

Routine is the enemy of originality,[1] and I see a teacher's duty as being to excite a joy in learning. As such, I am an unapologetic lifetime subscriber to the barmy. And the

---

[1]   I received a very angry letter about this phrase from someone who was clearly very clever. He described it as the kind of nonsense a 'beat poet' might come up with, pointing out that he had written four books, that the routine was 'crushing', but that without it he would not have been able to do so. I took his point. This is my fourth book.

barmy idea is this: arrange your classroom in a different way every day. It's just an idea but, you know, it might work!

In Defence of Front of Class Teaching

Funny old place America. In 2006 Oprah Winfrey played host to a teacher with a quite incredible story to tell: one Brad Cohen, winner of the (I kid you not) Howard Swearer Humanitarian Award and writer of the seminal tome, *Front of the Class: How Tourette Syndrome Made Me the Teacher I Never Had.*

Discovering the existence of this text led me to wonder what lessons might be like in Mr Cohen's class, and how great might be the pupils' whoops at the beginning of the year when they discover he is to be their teacher. You can bet there's never a dull moment in Brad's class; even if the subject he is teaching is dry, there's a cast iron guarantee that his delivery won't disappoint. Even if bored, students could indulge in a quick game of 'predict the profanity', and having teacher tic [*sic*] your book would take on a whole new meaning. The Tourette Syndrome Association of America, congratulating Brad on winning best educational book of 2005, notes that 'Brad still gets ejected from movie theatres and restaurants', but adds that he remains, of course, 'an inspiration to us all'.

Being ejected from public places is not an entirely unusual experience for educators. We are an odd lot. And this column is written in defence of those of us, like Brad, who stand in front of children and bravely manifest our naked eccentricities for their edutainment on a daily basis. Those of us who shamelessly still indulge in that near criminal, utterly subversive activity: front of class teaching.

I've noticed, since entering a profession I thought was called 'teaching', that what was such a central responsibility of the job that it gave it its name has been progressively devalued, as to be, in the view of the legislators, of almost marginal import. Teaching itself has been absented from the centre stage of our professional discourse, and replaced by the less easily quantified 'learning'.

Over the space of the last decade our professional expertise has, without our consent, seen a shift: we have gone from being specialists in 'teaching', to being slightly less expert in the broader field of 'teaching and learning' and, from thence, to being bewildered in the realms of the cumbersomely entitled 'learning and teaching'.

Numerous studies point to the fact that the bridge between teaching and learning is sometimes a bit rickety, and that what we might think of as great teaching doesn't necessarily result in the most learning.

Teaching and learning is a transaction that, if you think about it, has only four possible outcomes. The first and second show an easily understood cause and effect, either the teaching is good and kids learn stuff, or it's crap and they don't. There are instances, however, when the teaching is great and the kids learn nothing, or strangely, occasions when the teacher couldn't knock the pedagogical equivalent of the skin off a rice pudding but the kids still get multiple A stars.

The existence of the third of these, functional teaching–little learning, has caused the profession, rightly, to look at ways in which kids learn, and to add the word 'learning' to the equation.

The pivotal importance of learning admitted, it seems a logical step therefore, to reorder the responsibility, so that job adverts now advertise for Deputy Heads in charge of 'learning and teaching' in that order, and university faculties now have ridiculous new nomenclatures. This reordering shows a perverse misunderstanding of cause and effect – whilst teaching will often cause learning, learning will only in very sad circumstances cause teaching – and, as such, is nonsensical. It also has the effect of taking the teacher away from their position at the front of the class, transforming the role of teacher into that of facilitator, disinterested guide or, worse still, babysitter – and it may be seen as part of an attempt, conscious or otherwise, to devalue teaching as a craft or a professionalism.

If a teacher, rather than being a highly skilled artist, craftsperson or technician, expert in the 'million petalled flower' of teaching, is transmuted into a deskilled lackey facilitating learning, then it is children who will lose out. From our own schooling we remember, most of all, the charismatic madman, deliberately donning a coat of antic disposition, blowing things up at the front of the class. We remember the front of class teacher, and moreover, we remember his lessons and how excited we were to be in them. The foregrounding of learning over teaching is his death knell; a ringing that foretells also of a move towards serried ranks of students plugged into computers, supervised by an ICT technician.

So, I return in praise of Brad Cohen, whose book is called *Front of the Class*. Brad may well find it difficult to get served in a restaurant, but like the traditionalist head teacher who suggested to me, at the start of my career, that I do a lot of front of class teaching, he knows that the front is a good place for a teacher to stand. No matter what we are told by our betters, able teachers understand that they are, to quote Haim Ginott, 'the decisive element'. They know that while learning might sometimes happen accidentally, without great teaching it doesn't happen with any degree of regularity, or with much joy. Real teachers know that without them standing at the front of the class, delivering the knowledge, excitement, encouragement, passion and fun, schools will be very dull places indeed.[2]

---

[2] I'm not entirely sure about this conclusion. I have changed my own practice around this issue substantially since I wrote this. I think I have a point, but it should be substantially more nuanced than it appears here. (I am also aware that it is not entirely consistent with the previous article).

Pedagogy

Let's Plaster On a Fake Grin and Trawl through This Sorry Sack One More Time

When asked the name of the greatest man who ever lived, some would reach in the direction of Shakespeare, others might point towards Abraham Lincoln. Still more would go for Gandhi. A greater number, of course, would find even Gandhi's achievements pale when set against those of Sir Sidney James of the *Carry On* movies. I have a new candidate for this pantheon: Daniel Corbett.

Daniel Corbett is the BBC weatherman whose hands perform an entrancingly eloquent, disembodied ballet as he rhapsodises about cold fronts coming in from over the Pennines. There is a lot any teacher can learn from Daniel Corbett, not least through importing his techniques at that point when they share lesson objectives with the class. Rather than just trudge through the usual, perfunctory, tired and nasal monotone, 'Today, blah blah your lesson objectives blah blah blah,' Corbett's genius has injected new verve and passion into my presentation of these. I'll launch into his patented right-hand 'circle and flourish', the like of which you would normally expect from the multi-ringed hand of a French courtier, as I present to the class those most sultry and seductive of words, 'Today your lesson objectives are ...'

I do this, not only in tribute to Corbett, but also to hide the fact that importing the phrase 'lesson objectives' from the teaching manuals into the classroom is a bit dumb. During an inspection kids are meant to be able to tell OFSTED (Office for Standards in Education, Children's Services and Skills) inspectors what their lessons objective are. I've actually heard a conversation between one of my pupils and an OFSTED inspector.

'What's the lesson objective young man?'

'It's the thing the teacher has to put on the board, that we have to copy down because he can't be bothered to do a proper starter activity.'

'No, but what is an objective?'

'I told you ... It's the thing ... the teacher ... puts on the board. Strewth. Where did they get you from?'

'What are you learning today?' is another question entirely, and is likely to achieve a more satisfying response.

'What are we learning today? Oh we're learning about plate tectonics and oxbow lakes and the symbolic significance of the lighthouse in Virginia Woolf and the caves in Forster's *Passage to India*. You know, sir, I still have trouble in accepting Woolf as a feminist writer. But I can see you've got somewhere else to go to. There's always another teacher's career to be ruined. And it doesn't matter how poker faced you are, we know you're here to judge us, and assign all the work this brilliant human being has done in the last three years to change our lives for the better a near arbitrary and completely reductive grade.'

Teachers are meant to share lesson objectives at the beginning of each lesson, so that children have an explicit awareness about what it is that they are going to learn. That way, so the theory goes, they are involved in meta-cognition: thinking about learning, which is, apparently, a good thing for schoolchildren to be doing nowadays. Not actually learning, but thinking about it.

There are further controversies about lesson objectives, and the approach to these, from what I've seen, varies from school to school. In the school in which I spent most of my career we were expressly forbidden from using the verb 'know' in setting learning objectives. Woe betide the teacher who wrote, 'By the end of this lesson you will know something you didn't know before' on the whiteboard; he would be told off in a right royal manner. This foxed me. What's so wrong with knowing stuff? Isn't transmitting knowledge what we are paid to do? We'd be given voluminous lists of acceptable and unacceptable verbs to pin up on our classroom walls. 'Draw' was OK. 'Extrapolate' too. 'Learn', though, was most decidedly not.

It took me several years to work out why knowing and learning things in schools had been subject to such an evidently paradoxical pogrom. It was to encourage independent learning, this week's new fascism. You can 'know' something through the teacher talking about it for a whole hour. You can even 'learn' it that way. You can't draw it though. Know and learn were *verboten* in lesson objectives because it was tacit acceptance that the kids didn't have to do any work in order to know things, that you can transmit knowledge perfectly well through front of class teaching, and front of class teaching as all teachers now know, is very wrong indeed.

In some schools lesson objectives are differentiated, giving distinct likely levels of attainment by the end of the lesson. This works on a some–most–all formula. Some will be able to draw an archaeopteryx, most will have made some kind of mark on the paper, all will at least have picked up the pencil. For me, this way of doing things, though probably sound in principle, is a bit too nakedly open about the fact that the most one member of the class can manage is the odd dribble in a bucket.

The biggest question for me though with lesson objectives is why we have to share them at all. I can see why they have to be set. Without defining what the children are going to learn, you can just go through a series of unconnected exercises that pass the time quite adequately with no learning happening all year. But why the dictate that children must know what these are at the beginning of the lesson? Why can't we ask them to guess what they are going to learn, or tell us what they learnt at the end of the lesson? Why can't it be a surprise? Why all the 'if you don't do it this way you are an inadequate' strictures?

I dare any teachers reading this to try a week where you don't share lesson objectives at all with the pupils, and see what difference it makes to their learning. Letters, containing the phrase 'Sod all' to P. Beadle, care of *Education Guardian*.

Multiple Intelligences

John White, Emeritus Professor of Philosophy of Education at the Institute of Education, has recently published an essay calling Howard Gardner's multiple intelligences theory into question. Many of us in schools across the country use Gardner's theory as a guiding mechanism behind our classroom practice, and if Professor White has exposed it to be without foundation, then the world collapses and we are exposed as the frauds we've always suspected ourselves to be.

Gardner's theory has been virulent in schools. For those not in the education sector, Gardner proposes that intelligence is not limited to what we might call IQ, but is a collection of seven, eight or nine different intelligences. Logico-mathematical, linguistic, musical, spatial, bodily-kinaesthetic, intra-personal and inter-personal were the first batch. These have since been joined by naturalist and (perhaps) by existential.

In short, just because you're not good at maths and English it doesn't mean you're thick: you might have some other special ability, and this might usefully be termed an intelligence.

It's an immensely seductive measure for those of us working with students who find areas of the curriculum difficult to access. Helping a student discover what they are good at (or think/hope they're good at) and giving this the term 'intelligence' can have a marked effect on a child's self-esteem.

Some schools have even gone so far as to have 'smart' (or 'smarts') cards printed for students. A weird variation on donor cards, these say, 'Hi. I'm Mike, and I have high quotients of musical and logico-mathematical intelligence.' On seeing this, a teacher would know to avoid Mike as one would a leprous dog, since he likes nothing better than singing songs about sums, and is a nutter.

Professor White's arguments are many and complex. Loosely though, he suggests that Gardner's definitions of the varying intelligences have little to do with scientific fact, and are more the result of Gardner's own artistic judgement, superimposing his own previous studies in the arts onto Piaget's theories of development. The Professor also suggests that Gardner's criteria for defining an intelligence have been plucked from the ether; and the intelligences themselves don't even have to fulfil all such criteria.

He makes a compelling case. I too have had less academic worries than Professor White's about some of Gardner's theories: the definition of naturalistic intelligence for instance. Liking bunny rabbits and kittens is not a form of intelligence; more likely the obverse. Also, what is the difference between intra-personal and existential intelligence? Are the intra-personally intelligent deep thinkers and the existentially intelligent, like, really, really deep thinkers?

The notion of kinaesthetic intelligence is too broad. Anyone who's ever seen Frank Bruno poured into a tutu during panto season will tell you a boxer and a dancer aren't the same thing. Yet Gardner's theory will tell you that they possess high quotients of exactly the same intelligence.

When one comes to assessing students' intelligences with web-based tools, you often find these are creakier than an exam invigilator's Hush Puppies, and the questions you are required to answer are facile. Engaging in regular sporting activity is no measure of one's ability at it, and being asked whether you like 'all kinds of animals' is a question more suited to CBeebies than a serious scientific assessment.

White argues that Gardner's theory is developmentalist; that it proposes the existence of two polar states for each intelligence, the initial and the mature. The initial state is one's (alleged) genetic capacity for a certain intelligence; the mature state is less easily defined and, since there's no consensus as to how one would define it, relies on reference to cultural production. Gardner would argue that Keats, for instance, as a poet, would be an example of a mature linguistic intelligence.

But judging the maturity of this or that person's intelligence on the basis of their achievement or place in a near arbitrarily constructed canon is faulty. As is the notion that humans have a limited capacity set by a genetic code. Children are not hard-wired at birth. You can learn things. Jacqueline du Pré may not have been a particularly natural cellist, but you can bet your bum she practised a lot.

At its worst multiple intelligences can be used to deny the need to work at things. And, as such, can end up being just as reductive a form of labelling as the previous forms its application in schools seeks to overthrow. 'I don't have to work hard in maths, I'm musically intelligent.' I've even used it myself at home to justify lassitude. Claiming I don't have any visual intelligence has got me out of decorating the front room for a whole year now; it sometimes even gets me out of tidying up.

So there is much in Professor White's essay that makes sense. Where I baulk though is at any suggestion that schools should be throwing out effective practice because it is built on theoretical sand. Professor White says, 'If the intelligences are not part of human nature but wobbly constructions on the part of their author, educators should treat them with caution.'

It all depends on whether you as an educator protect notions of truth as being utterly sacrosanct. The aforementioned Keats's 'Ode on a Grecian Urn' contains the final couplet, '"Beauty is truth, truth beauty," – that is all ye know on earth, and all ye need to know.' This always struck me as romantic juvenile twaddle; and, to pervert a journalistic maxim, you should never let the truth get in the way of a good lesson.

Multiple intelligences works best as a model through which you can construct a really interesting lesson, or as a fairly advanced form of differentiation. Rather than getting the pre-literate students to fill out endless and pointless word searches and cloze procedures, get them to dance about it, sing about it, talk about it, think about it.

And whilst it may not be scientific fact that these intelligences exist, humans do possess different competencies. Judging an illiterate kid as thick, when in fact he can take a car engine apart and put it back together from memory, not only maims him – for life – but it is factually incorrect. Multiple intelligences may just be a sticking plaster to put on the gaping wounds of social exclusion, but it's the best thing we've got to hand as teachers.

As Gardner himself says, 'So long as materials are taught and assessed in only one way, we will only reach a certain kind of child. But everything can be taught in several ways. The more that we can match youngsters to congenial approaches of teaching, learning and assessing, the more likely it is that those youngsters will achieve educational success.'

So, is the theory of multiple intelligences flakier than a seven-day-old almond slice with dandruff? Quite possibly. But who cares?[3]

---

[3] John White's booklet *Howard Gardner: The Myth of Multiple Intelligences* is published by the Institute of Education in its Viewpoint series.

The Marshmallow Test

You pick up some odd pieces of knowledge as a freelance educationalist. Fascinating facts I have learnt this week are that hamsters are colour blind, the French for toad is *crapaud* and that the marshmallow has been around, in one form or other, for over two thousand years.

Which leads me to the partial theme of this month's column: the marshmallow test. In his book *Emotional Intelligence*, Daniel Goleman retells the story of a group of American scientists who created a specific torture for 4-year-olds. A scientist places a marshmallow on a table, telling the 4-year-old the scientist is off on an errand, and that if the child can resist the temptation to eat the marshmallow, they may gorge themselves on an extra one on the scientist's return. Some kids manage to resist temptation; some don't. The children are tracked and, 14 years later, their results in the marshmallow test prove to be a more reliable indicator of academic success than an IQ test. On leaving college those who had practised self-restraint and held out for the second marshmallow all became straight A students, whilst those unable to practise such superhuman self-control ended up as poly drug-addicted crazies.

Goleman takes this story as proof of the vast importance of self-regulation, or impulse control, the master aptitude of emotional intelligence. I have a different interpretation. The kids who resisted temptation were idiots! What kind of fool wastes 20 minutes of their life in torture for the sake of a single marshmallow? Eat the bloody thing the moment you are given it, and ask the scientist whether, since he is going on an errand, could he make a brief diversion to pick you up a family pack?

There are those who suggest we should incorporate teaching of the 'soft skills' of emotional intelligence, of which the marshmallow test is merely a whimsical illustration, into the curriculum, and cheap gags aside, I empathise with them.

This is an area where, for once, the real radicalism seems to be coming from the private sector. Dr Anthony Seldon's introduction last year of a well-being curriculum at Wellington College attracted a barrage of press attention, Ann Widdecombe hilariously describing it as 'the nanny state gone mad'. (Duh. Wellington is not a state institution.) The lessons, written by a Cambridge don, Professor Nick Baylis, and delivered by an absolute pearl of a teacher, Ian Morris, appear to be the start of a movement in British education. This month, over 200 head teachers, journalists and dignitaries attended a conference held at Wellington on the subject.

I travelled to the school earlier this year to sit in one of these happiness lessons, with one chief concern: that the lessons were being used as a sophisticated deflection tactic, permitting the school to pour ever more intense pressure on its pupils. Pop 'em the curricular equivalent of an anti-depressant, and you can get the boson to crack the whip all the harder.

However, suspicions that Seldon's intentions are in any way disingenuous are dispelled within seconds in his company. He explains, 'Teachers, like parents, want the children in their care to be mentally and physically healthy and intelligent in the roundest possible sense, and that's what teaching the skills of well-being is all about. Research and practice suggests it should be introduced in every school as a matter of priority.'

Whilst at the school, I interviewed the young men in year ten and, without exception, they claim to have enjoyed and benefited greatly from the lessons. If socially advantaged young men who spend their school years within Wellington's idyllic, wooded acres can benefit from such lessons, how great could the benefits be to those in less advantaged situations? Seldon acknowledges this: 'There is no more important objective for a school than to help its pupils find out who they are and how to lead happy and decent lives. The more deprived the area, the more vital this version of schooling is.'

Admittedly, financial straits are not the only form of poverty (it would be wrong to discount the emotional deprivation experienced by those at a boarding school like Wellington), but Seldon is right. The ability to recognise happiness when it occurs and to have it identified as something, perhaps the only thing, worth aspiring towards is not, as one critic has put it, Orwellian or Stalinist, but is a fundamental of decent schooling. If you don't know something exists then you cannot realistically aim for it. This applies equally to social mobility, which is also markedly absent from the curriculum. And at a time when the government is all too happy to criminalise children by trialling random drugs testing in some counties, then the pursuit of happiness lessons is surely worth a large scale trial itself.

Of course, you cannot promote social cohesion with missionary zeal alone, but people happy in themselves tend not to look too hard for scapegoats in other communities. So, if lessons in emotional intelligence and well-being are to find a way onto the curriculum, then where better to put them than in place of the failed citizenship experiment? Teaching kids how to be happy in themselves, and to empathise with each other, is surely more likely to promote social cohesion than teaching them to salute the flag, and if the marshmallow test is such a sure sign of future attainment, then a version of it should find its way onto the menu.

Get Yourself a System!

I met Barbara Windsor at a party recently. She told me that she knew who I was. This came as a surprise.

On the very same evening a television producer told me I was an 'intuitive' teacher, comparing me to the snub-nosed lady on the television who trains doggies. This also came as a surprise. I was offended. Not at someone comparing the children I teach to unruly canines, more at the idea of being thought intuitive.

Because intuitive is shorthand for sloppy, without a system. The intuitive teacher is a sixties throwback crying out to be rationalised, a long-haired liberal in need of a shave, a damn good haircut and a smart pair of slacks.

I determined to get ahead: to get myself a system.

After two hours in consultation with the world wide web I now know everything one needs to know. I have systems galore and some to spare. I know myself inside out and can label any pupil instantly.

Brett Bixler of Penn State University has designed a learning styles inventory that tells me I am a visual learner. The Learning Difficulties Pride website disagrees with Brett. They think that Brett is a charlatan and that I am obviously auditory. The good people at Red Rocks Community College grudgingly acknowledge both the auditory and visual parts of my make-up, but see through these fatuous illusions to the real kinaesthetic me.

Three different questionnaires surveying for the same thing come up with three opposing answers. This is hardly surprising given the kind of questions. Question 39 asks whether, 'When considering a body of information I am more likely to (a) focus on details and miss the big picture; or (b) try to understand the big picture before getting into detail?' I've pondered this and, in truth, have absolutely no idea whether I am a 'big picture' person or not. It isn't something I've ever thought of, nor, looking into the murky depths of my soul, do I think I will ever be able to come up with a judgement that holds any water at all.

It goes on to ask whether, when I meet people at parties, I am more likely to remember (a) what they looked like; or (b) what they said about themselves? Again, I don't know. I've only been to one party in the last five years and the only people who spoke to me were a television producer and Barbara Windsor. I remember both what Barbara said and what she looked like, but this is probably helped by the fact that *Carry On Camping* was the nearest thing to an erotic experience I had in the first 25 years of life.

But, as anyone who's completed a 'What kind of lover are you?' questionnaire in a red-top paper knows, they are addictive. I journeyed on in the hope I could find a church in which I could worship, a system that would truly fit.

Assessing my risk taking, I found I have a 76 percent risk type attitude. Exactly the same as Mr Blair's (though his sub-risk type is more rational than mine, and I am 1 percent more inspired than he). I wondered whether now would be the time to run for office and galloped in the direction of the Political Performance Indicator Tool. The results were disheartening. I score the same as both Stalin and Hitler, and less than Nero or Pol Pot; though I am more adventurous than either. Be afraid world.

As an entrepreneur I am only 10 percent inspired, but it was late and I wasn't feeling in an entrepreneurial frame of mind.

The Keirsey Temperament Sorter has sorted me out, and told me I am an idealist. North Carolina State University have me, like the faulty mirror, as being moderately reflective. I am finely balanced between sequential and global, visual rather than verbal, a distinctively expressed introvert and, God help me – not again – a completely intuitive learner.

There is even systematised self-help available for the poor intuitive type. We are advised that we are prone to careless mistakes on tests as we are impatient and don't like repetition. We must, 'take time to read the entire question and be sure to check [our] results'. Thanks for that.

In truth the whole escapade has left me absolutely bamboozled. I am no nearer knowing what my predominant learning style is, if I even have one, and seem, even after my search for system, to be forever tarred the slack intuitive.

Assessing students' learning styles, keeping the data and using it to plan lessons is, like the rest of the cod-psychological tosh on the web, a bucket full of balderdash. You cannot take a snapshot of someone's preferences on one day and use it to plan their whole future, as their responses are dictated by mood. Tomorrow, perhaps, I may be feeling more entrepreneurial, more kinaesthetic, more political, less intuitive. My answers, and consequently my profile, will be different.

The notion of personalised learning has excited many in the education world. It strikes the Department for Education and Skills (DfES) as a way forward. It worries me.

No teacher in the world has the time or technical ability to plan a lesson that is differentiated 30 ways. And you can have all the data in the world on a class: it doesn't mean you will be able to teach them.

The world of systematised learning is merely a means of selling computer software. Don't trust it. It is a set of crutches for the indolent of mind.

Better to trust in teachers' experience and professional judgement about what their class requires. Because if tuition is taken out of the realms of the teachers' intuition, if the word maverick continues to be used pejoratively and we are all judged on our ability to keep a spreadsheet of dubious data, then the poet Leonard Cohen was right: 'I have seen the future brother. It is murder. There won't be nothing you can't measure any more.'[4]

Of Seating Plans and Sealing Wax

I've started at a new school this academic year. It's scary, but nowhere near as scary as starting a whole new career as a newly qualified teacher (NQT). What you don't have in starting a school as a relatively experienced teacher is the fear that, no matter how intense your life experiences have been, no matter how many bar room brawls you've lost, no

---

[4] It is a source of much irritation to me that the real lyric to this song, 'The Future', is, 'There won't be nothing you *can* measure any more,' which is nowhere near as good.

matter how many cracked teeth you've got, you won't be able to cut it in the classroom.[5]

What you do have to take away any of such angst is a finely honed seating plan.

Now you might imagine that the seating plan is a fairly dry – nay, positively sarcastic – subject for a newspaper article: you might be right. Seating plans aren't the glamour end of the business, but when on the first day of a new job you are greeted with a student who is a whole foot taller than you, who doesn't like the way you just looked at him and who is a semi-professional power-lifter, then they're vital.

You can simply point at the nicely hand-drawn piece of paper with their name on it, grunt, and then point at the place where they are to sit for the rest of the year. School students know in their heart-of-hearts that the teacher is allowed to tell them where to sit, and will skulk off muttering half-heard profanities in the direction of their chair. Which is as far away from their mates as they can possibly be, without standing outside. Or in another school. In another country.

Last year, I attempted to get a bit of in-school research going about this very subject, sending my colleagues a patronising questionnaire (which, since I am not a senior manager I rarely get the opportunity to do). These were duly returned (only one ruined ballot: stained with something strange) and most responses seemed to stress the importance of flexibility. Responses such as, 'I like mine flexible and easy to change,' came generally from the female members of staff. I tutted like an old lady in a strip club on reading this;

---

[5] Oh, the hubris. I actually got torn to shreds by a year nine class in this school. The reason? Firstly, not being as good as I thought I was. Secondly, I let them negotiate the seating plan.

the seating plan's rigidity, and its progenitor's utter inflexibility in enforcing it, is in many ways its reason for being.

'Please sir, can I sit next to my mate?'

'Nope.'

'I work better with ...'

'Nope.'

'When can we move seats?'

'Never. Never. Never.'

As part of the research, and seeing as girls have been out-performing boys in my subject – English – since Plato was at the chalkboard, I wondered whether there was a way in which one could arrange the classroom in a mixed school to help the boys out a bit. It turns out there is.

One of the issues that affects boys in particular is the desire not to be seen as thick. By trying hard when surrounded by girls who will often – in English lessons at least – be achieving far higher grades than them, boys make themselves more vulnerable than they would like to be. And if they can't be seen to be doing well by their peers, they will often gain the cool points by letting it appear that they don't give a toss.

Girl-boy-girl-boy seating plans are great for ensuring behaviour's in the right region, but they don't much help the boys' academic achievement unless ...

Unless you sit boys with girls of slightly lower attainment. Level seven boys will sit with level six girls, level six boys with level fives, and so on. Your cleverest girls then sit on the same table as the boys who require the most help, which often high-attaining girls will be most willing to provide (all the ladies love a bad boy). This way the boys get to feel good about themselves as they are the ones doling out the help and advice. They are the ones whose chests are puffed with pride at their possession of superior knowledge. (God! Blokes! I'm glad I'm not married to one.)

Of course this is a model; real classrooms don't divide along such easy lines. But it is a model that takes into account academic achievement instead of behaviour. Often, we as teachers are so scared of poor behaviour that we forget the best way of ensuring it doesn't crop up is making sure everyone's learning. Kids know what they're at school for. And they like learning. Honest.

Another thing to keep in mind is ethnicity. Often in multi-cultural schools like will gravitate to like, so that all the black boys sit on one table, Asian girls at the next. I left things to chance with my year tens last year, and eventually we were left with a multi-cultural classroom in which there was one last dying bastion of empire; what we jokingly referred to as 'the white supremacy table'. I felt sad for the children huddled together under the flag of St George. I felt they were missing out on something, and eventually I rearranged the way students were sat, keeping in mind their right to mix with, and learn from, people of different cultural origin.

So, if the only thing swinging in your classroom at the moment is your ego in a noose, now is a good time of year to change things. Enforcing a new seating plan after the autumn half-term sets new boundaries, and gives everyone (not least the teacher) a chance of a fresh start.

Imagine, if you would, that you are getting married. Two of your friends used to go out with each other. They've since split up, and the discarded party – out of thwarted love – now hates their ex-partner with psychotic passion; and has threatened to do over the ex's new love. You have to invite both parties, but you're not going to sit them on the same table, unless you're a complete dunce. There may well be a teenage version of this scenario being enacted in your classroom without your knowledge, and you'd be wise to remember that preventative measures, at all times, trump the curative.

Key Words

A couple of years ago they were all the rage. Every lesson had to have at least a few. Staffrooms buzzed with the concept. Lesson plans still feature an apologetic little section on which to record them. Caretakers spent half their lives erecting special boards for teachers to display them. Schools hand out expensively produced, colour-coded folders for kids to keep them in. Yes, children: the key words for this lesson are 'key' and 'words'.

Whilst the sharing of key words is not part of the structural strictures of the government's recommended four-part lesson, there is an unwritten rule in most classes, primary or secondary, that each lesson must feature a few of them. But key words themselves are the subject of some confusion in the profession – we are told we must have them, but there is little direction from on high as to when, why, what or how.

Let's take the 'when' first. Many teachers share key words as a part of the starter activity they've been told must take place at the beginning of every lesson. The problem with the introduction of key words as part of a starter, aside from the obvious fact that starter activities themselves are simply a pointless exercise in creation of work for the already overburdened, is that this technique leads educators to grope desperately and inevitably in the direction of the word search. Many teachers will waste the lunchtime they could have been eating both a sandwich and a banana piecing together a word search incorporating the lesson's key words. Some even go so far as to produce worksheets featuring anagrammatic versions.

This is a whole hill of effort for a ten-minute starter that may engage some low-end version of cognition, but teaches neither concept, information, idea nor any skill – other than doing pointless anagrams (a skill not conspicuous for its appearance on too many person specifications I've ever seen, nor of much use at parties).

I've occasionally ventured an admittedly controversial opinion that student teachers, on picking up their qualified teacher status, should then be escorted to the Department of Schools and Families' (DCSF) resident team of tattooists. There they would be inscribed with an inconspicuous tattoo on the inside of their right wrist (it doesn't need to be too obtrusive: we are not talking about a full-face spider web or a burka here). The tattoo says, 'No one ever learnt anything from a bloody word search.' The word ever is underlined.

If key words as starters are pedagogically flawed, then the other obvious time at which to share them is after the teacher has spouted the lesson objectives at their charges. 'Today, children, we are learning how to properly conjugate the past tense of the verb "to be", that's right, "I was, you was, we was", and your key words for this lesson are "was" and "was".' This seems the logical place to me. It is the guided part of the lesson, and the teacher is introducing new information.

The 'why' is obvious. It is a key part of a teacher's role to introduce children to new vocabulary. Often, when asked what I do for a living, I'll either reply that I am a children's entertainer or, more accurately, that I teach kids big words with which to annoy their parents. Until you've heard a year ten student in an inner city school describe themselves as an 'anti-Freudian nihilist', then you haven't lived, and it is this second version of my job description, I think, that is what teachers are paid to do: to give children access to the vocabulary that will act as a passport to new worlds.

This links to the 'what'. Key words are meant to be high order, subject specific, new vocabulary. Enjambment is a key word. Bucket is not. I have lost count of the number of times I have sat in science lessons where the key word was bucket. Bucket is not an appropriate key word. It is a bucket. They are different.

It's the 'how', however, which is the key to useful teaching of key words. Often teachers will display these, and make no mention of their meaning. Kids will copy the words down into special folders at the beginning of every lesson over a period of three years, so that by the end of key stage three they have a bulging collection of pages in an A5 ring binder, scribed with a vast collection of words, and not so much as a note as to their meaning. Key word folders are very much the kind of thing that a ten-minute OFSTED inspection would make positive remark upon but, again, where's the learning?

For me, the sharing of the key words was always the most vital part of the lesson. Share the objectives (if you can be arsed), forget the starter and plough straight into intro- ducing, then defining, the new vocabulary for the lesson. This section of the lesson was always so vital to me, that I'd often lose myself in some absurd drama activity defining 'empathetic' and forget entirely to hand out the pointless, functional, 'keep 'em shut up' worksheet.

The definition of new vocabulary could take any form the teacher wishes. As with everything in education the only limit is the teacher's imagination. I would argue though that teachers who do not see the introduction of new vocabulary as one of the most exciting parts of the job are missing out. Key words are not just the secondary version of the weekly spelling test. They are not simply objects to be displayed on colourful paper replicating the disembodied words in the key word folders. They are, as genius primary practitioner Ros Wilson says, 'wow' words, special vocabulary enhancing children's lives. They should be treated with reverence.

The State Approved Method of Instruction

Starter – guided – independent – plenary – dung. 'One of these things', to quote the old *Sesame Street* song, 'does not belong here, one of these things is not the same.' The first four are the sequence the DfES recommends teachers follow for more or less every lesson; the fifth might profitably be employed as a collective noun for the other four in sequence.

The literacy and numeracy hours in primary schools were set up on a similar model and, since the introduction of these seem to have paid DfES dividends (the educational equivalent of Mr Forsyth's Brucey Bonus) in terms of SATs results, this model of teaching was rolled out across key stage three, and from thence onwards; until such point that it is now perceived in many schools as the only acceptable model for teaching.

You may well baulk righteously about the idea of an 'acceptable' or 'appropriate' style of teaching but, briefly, the four-part lesson works (or doesn't) like this: you tell children what they are going to learn (if you really want to waste some time you can get them to copy it off the board), then you do some completely unrelated ten-minute activity which took an hour to prepare. After spending 20 minutes tidying this up, you launch – half an hour into the lesson – into teaching them something. In theory, your class would then apply this knowledge independently, but you took too much time on the starter, till, at the end you do a recap in which you ask your class what they have learnt, and they reply, 'Nothing. We spent most of the lesson tidying up the Scrabble boards.'

Simple really. The phrase four-part lesson plan is controversial in some parts. For many it goes together with good teaching like a horse and gherkin,[6] and is just one more symptom of modern education's inexorable path towards being its own antithesis. It is a process through which the genius of teaching can be homogenised into mechanistic mediocrity. You wouldn't invite a master carpenter into your house to do some work and tell him he wants to get rid of all that fancy joinery and put the shelves up with Evo-Stik; why then are experienced teachers told that they must follow such a reductive and simplistic formula?

At its best, the four-part lesson plan guarantees a modicum of pace; only the most blindingly slack teacher will have sufficient brass neck or style to write a four-part lesson plan

---

[6] I am not sure this metaphor works. What if horses like gherkins?

which records the following activities: 'starter: word search', 'guided: how to copy off the board', 'independent: intense copying off the board', 'plenary: how might we improve copying off the board?' There is at least the small guarantee that there will be some variety in the lesson. But, at its worst, it's a dunce's dictate: a structure with which you can almost guarantee a mediocre lesson. The four-part lesson plan promotes and rewards bad teaching; teaching which is routine, formulaic; teaching which thoughtlessly hands out a lot of photocopied worksheets; teaching in which there is no room to run with some brilliant idea that just occurred to a pupil, because we, a set of fantastically creative professionals, are scared of being ticked off by someone who is better at unquestioningly obeying stupid rules than us.

A good teacher may well use some model with which to structure the learning of their pupils. I have had some success with using Gardner's multiple intelligences theory as a model for a seven-part lesson: write about it, calculate it, sing it, dance it, think about it, talk about it, paint a picture of it ... until such point as Gardner extended the intelligences to include naturalistic and existential, and now we have to spend the plenary outside relating everything to God. A confident teacher might plan a lecture that takes a week to deliver, followed by a lesson with 25 separate two-minute activities. How's about that for pace, Mr Inspector?

But the point is each teacher has their own unique style. The four-part lesson plan is only of use as a default setting for the sort of bread-and-butter, run-of-the-mill lesson on a wet Tuesday that both teacher and pupils have already forgotten before it has started. The moment the individual teacher has a better idea, one about which they are enthused and can enthuse their charges, they should go off-piste and follow their nose to where the real learning is.

It is no coincidence that the idea of an acceptable or appropriate, or even ideologically pure, model of teaching flourished and grew at the point that Standartenführer Woodhead was in charge of the enforcement arm of the standards police; and questions have been raised as to whether there is a broader political agenda behind this.

This is an interesting rumble, which appears to have been proved right. Many teachers would have you believe that the four-part lesson plan is a move to standardise to such an extent that any damn fule can deliver a lesson. It seeks to take the element of professional judgement out of teaching, so that it is no longer a graduate job, and lessons can be delivered by teaching assistants.

Teaching assistants do fantastically valuable jobs supporting children who desperately need and have an entitlement to that support, and it is vital to those children's progress that they are not deployed away from their side. But teaching assistants currently command sweatshop salaries, and if teaching is reduced to a formula so simple that you require no serious training to do it, then it makes sound sense to the paymasters that it is done as cheaply as possible.

Many teachers wheel out the four-part lesson plan when observed. There is such a climate of fear and pressure towards conformity in many schools that teachers will exercise the full realm of their skills only when safely locked away with their classes, and will reduce what they do to bland conformity when open to public scrutiny. If I have words of advice for such teachers, it is don't bother.

The four-part lesson plan is part of a process to deskill you to such an extent that you will be replaced as an educator by someone who benefited little from education themselves. If the DfES continues to believe that teachers blindly follow such an absurd dictate, they will take it as your acquiescence to a generation of children being taught only by people with no professional or subject expertise.

Hands Up!

Hands up who thinks the practice of asking for hands up in school is wrong. Scans the room. No hands. Waits the suggested 30 seconds. Scans again. Still no takers.

The DfES has issued guidance suggesting that the practice of asking for hands up in class leaves many kids in school behind, and whilst the Department has added the magnificently ironic caveat, 'We would categorically never prescribe what teachers do in their own classrooms,' there is definitely the suggestion that the teacher-led discussion has had its lard, and we shouldn't really be using it any more.

The reason for this is that, as any teacher will tell you, it is always the same five or six pocket battleship-sized egos coming up with the answers; the rest of the class are left mute and, in our collective teacher-paranoia, we suspect the quiet kids are completely unengaged. Or are they? Ian Gilbert in the preface to his *Little Book of Thunks: 260 Questions to Make Your Brain Go Ouch*, puts forward a dissenting view: 'Just because they are not talking doesn't mean they're not joining in. Far from it. Sometimes those who speak most think least. It's the same in the pub.'

Predictably, the DfES's guidance has been ridiculed in some parts as being both pointless and gormless, many wilfully confusing the suggestion that a teacher-led discussion may not always be the best way of prompting debate with a dictate that children must nevermore raise their hands in class, or they'll get 'em chopped off. As per usual, it is the 'it never did me any harm' brigade making the most noise: teacher-led discussion has been a favoured method of instruction since children were first allowed to speak in class and experienced teachers don't need telling how, or even whether, to use such a key tool in their armoury.

Or do they? The fact that this technique has been a fundamental in a teacher's toolkit since Plato was a twinkle in his Dad's one good eye shouldn't necessarily mean that it should remain there. Tools become outmoded: we don't use sheep's jawbones to kill swine any more, nor do we go to war sporting longbows. There are manifold issues with the primacy of this form of instruction in our classrooms, not the least of which being that it is really, very, bloody difficult to get right.

Witness the technique used by many an NQT to start such a discussion. Firstly, clap your hands together and say, 'OK.' Wait a second and observe the children carrying on their conversations regardless. Clap hands together again and, in a slightly louder voice, mouth 'OK' again, but this time add the suffix 'then' to let them know you really mean business. Wait a second and note the fact that the noise has died down ... not one bit. Then reach for the Exocet. Bang the desk with the flat palm of the hand, rupturing a tendon in the process, and in a near shout ruefully intone the word, 'Right.' Take note of the one head in the class which turns slightly towards you, before going straight back to his conversation.

Many an NQT has entered the profession assuming that leading discussion is an area in which they'll soon sprout wings and fly towards excellence, only to find out that they are ritually slaughtered by classes when they try. Turn your back for a minute to record a pupil's thoughts on the board and you'll find paper flying everywhere; you can attempt to open the discussion a hundred times before any of the little buggers allow you to speak, and it seems to be one of those activities which prompts many boys' hands to go into automatic drumming monkey mode. Running a discussion well is, perhaps, the most technically complex of all teaching techniques, and is the metaphorical rock on which many a fledgling career has run to ground. You must be prepared to insist on utter silence before launching into the debate, ensure that no one is so much as even thinking about holding a pen and be prepared to turn a kindly eye to those irritating kids who do the 'I'm going to wet myself' dance in their chair to ensure you ask them their opinion first.

Gilbert ably satirises another issue with the teacher-led discussion as practised in many schools, suggesting it is actually a thinly veiled version of a traditional and meaningless game by the name of 'Guess what's in the teacher's head?'

Even with the use of skilled questioning techniques to avoid this, for me the key issue is that in a class discussion very few people get to express themselves, and this is where the DfES's guidance is, I think, welcome. What is the point of undertaking an exercise in which only a few children ever take part? Organising discussion is an area where the teaching profession has revealed itself to be as creative as it claims. We have come up with the goods here time after time. The existence of paired discussion, trios, talking in groups, jigsaws, pairs to fours, expert groups, argument tunnels, verbal tennis or any of the other fantastic techniques that are readily available with only the slightest bit of interest in how to teach, takes the teacher away from the front of the class and gives all students a forum in which they might express themselves and develop their oracy skills. These techniques, unlike the reliable old teacher-led discussion, actually promote independent learning and, in taking the teacher away from the front, take him away from both the potential for being abused, as well as away from his position as the only source of knowledge in the room. There is really no reason, other than lack of preparation time, laziness or fear of noise for any teacher to bother with leading a 'hands-up half-hour'.

Mind Maps

I mind mapped this article before writing it. It would be interesting to find out whether regular readers noticed any rinse in quantity [*sic*].

Mind mapping is easy. Firstly, you have to locate hundreds of coloured pencils, then, in a scene reminiscent of a particularly sadistic detention in a 1970s primary school, you sharpen them until your right index finger is swollen and covered in coloured graphite.

Of course the leads will become lodged in the sharpener, which will then break, but you must persist. Under no circumstances ever use a felt tip.[7] They are wrong.

Turn your paper landscape style, then draw something right dead bang in the middle. Do not go near the sides children for we are 'radiant' thinkers and need space to spread our thoughts! Take six multi-coloured lines out and draw a picture at the end of each one that is in some way related to the central picture. The lines should be affectedly curly: there is no room for the ruler in the realms of the creative.

---

[7] This piece of advice is wrong. Felt tips are very good indeed for mind maps.

Finally, write key words in upper or lower case on the curly lines. You have now drawn a basic mind map and are ready to rule the world and the spineless ants that inhabit it.

Mind maps have all the seductiveness of any piece of popular science – when we have mastered them we feel as if we are in possession of a piece of complex information that few own (just the select few million who have purchased a book by their progenitor, the stupendously wealthy Tony Buzan). And they come with some grand claims: mind maps 'help make your life easier and more successful', says Buzan in *How to Mind Map*. You will immediately 'think up brilliant ideas' and 'gain control of your life'. Given these claims, which stop just short of declaring the mind map the solution to war, pestilence and famine, it is a wonder that the world managed to turn without them. In employing the language of the snake oil salesman, Mr Buzan causes the sentient to doubt whether mind maps are intended for anyone other than the mentally infirm. Teachers are generally sentient. Mind maps bring out the staffroom cynic in all of us.

The popular science bit of them is this. Your brain has two hemispheres, left and right. The left is the organised swot who likes bright light, keeps his bedroom tidy and can tolerate sums. Your right hemisphere is your brain on drugs: the long haired, creative type you don't bring home to mother.

According to Buzan, orthodox forms of note taking don't quite stick in the head because they only employ the left brain, the swotty side, leaving our right brain, like many creative types, sitting kicking its heels on the sofa, watching underclass TV and waiting for a job offer that never comes. Ordinary note taking – apparently – puts us into a 'semi-hypnotic trance state'. (Which some would say is a good thing.) In short, they don't properly reflect our patterns of thinking, and so don't properly aid recall. Buzan's arguments for his invention are that using images taps into the brain's key tool for storing memory; and that the process of creating a mind map uses both hemispheres.

The trouble is that such lateralisation of brain function is scientific fallacy,[8] and a lot of Buzan's thoughts seem to rely on the old, 'We only use 10 percent of the neurons in our brain at one time' nonsense. He is selling to the bit in all of us that imagines ourselves to be potential super powered, probably psychic, hyper intellectuals. There is a reason we only use 10 percent of our neurons at one time. If we used them all simultaneously we would not, in fact, be any cleverer. We would be dead, having first enjoyed a massive seizure.

It is a shame that perfectly good teaching tools continually have to be justified with such hokum reference to neuro science. Teachers are interested in things that have useful practical application. If we wanted to be walking authorities on the hippocampus and cerebellum we would have got better A levels and worn slightly more conservative clothes.

The mind map is probably underused in schools because of its associations with bad science and low order marketing. Many teachers believe Mr Buzan is actually wearing a new pair of underpants and that you can see his winky through them. But don't believe the hype. Providing you have access to a whole ship full of coloured pencils and a naughty boy to sharpen them, they are a good and valid classroom method with a variety of applications. The educationist Ian Gilbert's book *Essential Motivation in the Classroom* tells a possibly

---

[8]   Here I am the idiot. It is hemispheric dominance that is fallacy; lateralisation of brain function is accepted scientific fact. I wish *Guardian* writers would do their homework.

apocryphal story of a school in which revision notes were all in the form of mind maps. Come exam time, teachers erected a giant white screen and asked students to project their recollections of their revision notes onto it. Needless to say everyone got an A* and world peace was finally achieved.

As visual tools, they have brilliant applications for display work that at least appears to be more cognitive than colouring in a poster. They look smashing, and I think it is fairly indubitable that using images helps recall. If this is the technique used by the memory men who can remember 20,000 different digits in sequence whilst drunk to the gills, then it's got to be of use for year eight bottom set.

Problems with them are that visual ignoramuses, such as this writer, can't think of that many pictures and end up repeatedly drawing question marks where detailed representations of a frog should be. The borderline autistics amongst us can also get stuck for hours on choosing which of the hundreds of different coloured pencils at their disposal they should use. They are no good as planning tools for those with a linguistic bias, as the process of creating one is too bloody slow and, probably because of all the left-brain-right-brain-cross-filtration-action, they can actually give you a headache.

But they are a useful piece of any teacher's repertoire, given the right circumstances. I have always had a particular fondness for one of my father's tools. It is called a podger, and it does just that: it podges. There comes a time when you are burning off bolts that it is the only thing that will do. It's a useful tool the podger but, like the mind map, you shouldn't mistake it for a universal screwdriver.

Brainless Gym

Does anybody remember the thing you'd do in primary schools, where you would pat your head and rub your stomach at the same time? Apparently, it's a science, and it has a name. It's called Brain Gym and no, you don't have to attach weights to your cerebellum; Brain Gym is a combination of prescribed movements which, so we are told, leave students in a relaxed state, ready to soak up more information about oxbow lakes. There are specific moves for when a child is depressed, or for when they are upset. Don't worry reader, I am laughing as I type this.

I've invented a couple of my own exercises on this theme. First, trace the fingers of your right hand, from the top of your back, to the bottom, one vertebra at a time. Once you have reached the bottom vertebrae, slide your right hand underneath it. This is your arse. Now place your left hand on your right shoulder (which, apparently, improves brain laterality). When you have done this look directly down. This is your elbow. Do not confuse the two.

I'll be putting the exercise into book form along with some generic illustrations of smiling children. I call the activity 'brainless gym' and I am available to teach it to other teachers at exorbitant rates throughout June and July.

Dr Ben Goldacre, self-styled 'serious, f***-off academic ninja' and owner of a first class honours degree in medicine from Magdalene College, Oxford, stirred up a hornet's nest recently with his claims in *The Guardian* that Brain Gym is pseudoscience. The article has, so far, generated 282 comments on Ben's website (www.badscience.net), and the controversy has been so intense that I can well imagine a post-nuclear future in which primary teachers will be asked whose side they were on when the Brain Gym wars raged. The comments range from people supporting Ben's position that teachers who actually teach the kids the pseudoscientific codswallop behind Brain Gym should be sacked (a bit harsh), to those happy to provide anecdotes of its success with their students.

Part of the controversy that has raged has been the result of wilful misunderstanding on the part of some of the teachers. Brain Gym is, in essence, pretty sensible. It suggests that children should be properly hydrated to perform well, and that a bit of physical activity in the middle of a lesson can wake kids up. The good doctor does not disagree with this. His issue is with what I described in last month's column as being the 'hokum references to neuroscience'. Some teachers have reacted strongly to this, concluding erroneously that Dr Goldacre is against hydration and exercise.

He isn't. For those teachers who are not too good at comprehension, Ben clarifies: 'Just to make it even clearer: stopping and doing some exercise is good, lying to children with bonkers pseudoscientific explanations is bad.'

Dr Goldacre's position is crystal clear. His issue is with what Dr Barry Beyerstein, a Professor of Psychology at Simon Fraser University in Burnaby, Canada, describes as 'commercial ventures promoted by hucksters who mislead consumers into thinking that their products are sound applications of scientific knowledge'. Or the patronising rubbish remarked upon by Sheffield psychologist, Andy Brown, where teachers are shown PowerPoint presentations of brains growing next to a watering can.

The claims behind Brain Gym are quite obviously so silly they would make a bullmastiff dislocate his lower jaw with laughter. I am not a fully fledged, properly trained, licensed

Brain Gym trainer. Nor ever will be. I've actually only used it twice. Both times there were television cameras present. It is the kind of flashy nonsense that translates well on screen and impresses the great British public as it makes the kids laugh. And this is where I'd defend it. It's fun. If children are bored with the work, listless and grumpy, it's a way of injecting a bit of energy into the room. What works about it specifically is they can do a bit of physical exercise without invading each other's personal space, falling into each other or bashing each other up. The exercises are discrete, don't use up a lot of space and are focused on the self.

But there are other ways of doing this, for which you don't have to buy into the cod neuroscience. Fidget time is quite a laugh. If the kids are getting fidgety, allow it. Give them an allocated two minutes in which to fidget, and join in. Chair dancing works fantastically as well. Bung some Michael Jackson on the stereo, and get them to dance with only their top halves whilst still seated. There is no science behind this whatsoever: it's just a laugh.

And this is, perhaps, where Ben, who is a doctor and had little experience of schools, mistakes posterior and joint. Teachers don't believe any of the tumperymoonshine about Brain Gym: it's more full of holes than a ten-day-old snot rag. In reality, we are all sat at the INSET sessions where some Brain Gym guru takes us through the moves, hiding behind our hands, sniggering in disbelief. And moreover, if we do submit to the sales patter and ever use the techniques such self-appointed gurus teach us, none of us would even think of teaching the claptrap behind it. Neuroscience, good or bad, is not on the curriculum of any school I know. And teachers don't indoctrinate children with lies willingly. Usually we save the lies for either our next performance development review, or the students' predicted GCSE grades.

As Ben suggests, you'd probably get as much benefit from taking a Brain Gym book and booting it around the room. Force feeding litres of water to children during class will lead to 30 children wanting to go to the toilet in unison, and there is, of course, a decent argument for, rather than indulging in a series of stretching exercises when you should be doing some work, actually, erm, continuing doing the work.

Marking

There is a recognised psychological condition that goes by the name of 'erotographomania': the obsessive desire to write love letters. If you leave aside the piteous chuckles for a moment, it's possible to picture the havoc such an illness could wreak on a person's life.

Imagine then, if you will, the poor victim of that equally virulent illness, Orexis Paginaperlegere, the obsessive desire to correct the work of another.

Being a teacher has led me into some ridiculous patterns of behaviour. For instance, I am unable to read a newspaper article without marking it. I read reviews of records I will never have the time to hear, of art forms in which I have no interest and, as I read, I emit a tut: 'Tsk, no comma after adverbial sentence start. B-. See me.' Or 'Heavens-to-Betsy! What a charming subordinate clause. Stout feller!' I have become, in short, a pint-sized, East End version of Lynne Truss (minus the royalty cheques, worldwide fame and the odd lie-in).

I am also afflicted with a particularly debilitating and extremely specialist teacher paranoia, Consternatio rubrum stilum amittere – the fear of misplacing your red pen. I am no longer, in social situations 'Y'know, Phil, the funny bloke with the curly hair'. I am now 'Mr Beadle – you know, that knackered-looking feller with the collection of red pens in his top pocket ... and not much hair'.

But still I remain evangelical about the subject of marking. Evangelical, not in the sense that I get out the tambourines when a pupil places a semicolon correctly, though I don't discount the idea; more in the sense that marking is a subject on which I am not averse to mounting the pulpit.

So, dog collar on, I'll don the ecclesiastical vestments, and with a mighty 'Hosannah' impart the word: marking books is actually fun![9]

I'm aware of how silly this might sound to overburdened teachers, particularly those with a specialism in English, but it's true. Marking, say the naysayers, transforms creative, passionate individuals into careworn members of the drudge squad. For many teachers, Hephaestus' lot seems entirely manageable. Marking is hard to do, you're always behind and it never, ever stops.

Far better the token tick, the cursory 'well done' and the evening in front of the telly than lifting your heavy – nay, cadaverous – head yet again from a pool of spittle and yelling tiredly, 'Once more into the book, my friend', staining yet another poor student's beautifully presented work with slashes and swathes of blood-like ink. Would you want to read Kylie's 24-page long, unparagraphed fairytale featuring character names and romantic aspirations nicked from *EastEnders*? It's a tough trawl baby.

---

[9]   I find these last two paragraphs unbearably pompous.

But it's worth doing.

If you've got the stomach for it, you'll find something in Kylie's story that'll make you cry. Or laugh out loud. Or both.

I mark predominantly between the hours of seven – on a good day – and nine in the morning. Whilst I'm often bleary at such hours, the prospect of communing with the work of the school's nascent novelists is generally enough to get me out of bed with some kind of paunchy bounce.

I think it was Charles Bukowski who described the central tragedy of human existence as being that 'Every man is born a genius, but dies a fool'. And, if this is true – which it is – then reading the poetic works of 11-year-olds is surely one of the most obvious paths there is to enlightenment.

This week alone, Abie in year eleven has described her anger as being 'a purple flower'; Sigrida's poetry requests that the reader 'Hide my name, un-name my breath and speak of air, in which I do not live'; and Patrick, a genius whom I count myself lucky to have known, has constructed a morality tale based upon the disembodied adventures of a French teacher's moustache and its dislike for seventies tank-tops and the word 'anus'.

If you pick up a pen, you are a writer. An unread writer is that forlorn tree in the forest that no one hears fall. There is nothing more frustrating and disappointing, nothing more likely to disenchant the young writers in our schools, than their reader – the teacher – failing to pick up their work and notice its brilliance. So do it. Do it every day. Do it with a smile. And do it knowing it's worth doing well.

The question is, how on earth does one do it well? Here are some cunning tricks.

With regard to targets, the key to a student's progress, there's a quick and sure-fire way of getting these set. There will be mistakes in the first paragraph. No matter how brilliant your student, there will be something in their first few sentences – a forgotten apostrophe, an overused discourse marker – that is worthy of remedy. When first looking into Chapman's essay, leave a space for the effusive praise, set down two targets, and then go back to reading the work.

While proofing every single word, you construct the nice things you are going to say about your student's tome. Don't over-praise, but there's nothing wrong with encouragement. Pick your favourite bit, and say why – exactly why – you liked it. Acknowledge the writer as a human being who has both exceptional and unique thoughts, profound feelings and sensibilities. Form a marking relationship; you might even want to comment on their quite astounding taste in footwear and jewellery. Bung an effort and GCSE grade on it and you're done. On to the next book ...

Marking is the secret and special relationship between teacher and student. It is not in the public realm. You can't accidentally humiliate a child by privately praising what they have written.

My own devotion to the gospel of marking is the sole reason that the children I teach regard me as being a 'good' teacher. If you have a naughty boy or girl, it is also the best way to their heart. And, with the possible exception of being gentle to children whose lives sometimes set them too great a challenge to bear, it is the single most important thing a teacher does.

Any fool can come up with a five-step lesson plan (formulated in the five steps before you get to the classroom door), but a teacher who knows exactly who their children are, and what it is they need to learn, is a teacher who is armed with fistfuls of magic and gold.

Assessment for Learning

At the beginning of the spring term in 2006, I left the classroom for two-and-a-bit years of swanning around, making telly programmes and writing a mass-market book that was substantially less mass market than the publishers had intended. I didn't return until February last year. In the winter term of 2005, the phrase on everyone's lips was 'assessment for learning'. Not assessment of learning. No. That was passé, even in 2005. The school I was working in at the time was going to 'drive up standards through assessment for learning'.

At the time, I understood the distinction and didn't think I'd have to alter my practice substantially. I was already doing it (so I thought). Mark their books, see what they don't know and teach them it. It seemed not only simple, but that the world was shifting slowly my way, since that was what I did every morning. On marking the books, I'd realise that not a single pupil I had taught could master the possessive apostrophe (impossible to teach) and, accordingly, I'd teach them it that day. Of course, it made for dull lessons and uninspired pupils, but it made lesson planning easy, and didn't seem to get in the way of being seen as good at the job.

'What are we learning today, sir?'

'The possessive apostrophe.'

'But we learned that yesterday.'

'No. You didn't.'

'You're a crap teacher, sir.'

'Thank you. I know.'

Returning to the game last year, I was struck by how assessment for learning (AfL) has become a viral philosophy. It infiltrates every corner of every mention of school improvement, and seems to be accepted on tablets written on stone as, perhaps, the single most important key to pupil achievement. But until last term I had no idea what it was. 'Mark their books properly' is vastly too unsophisticated an understanding of a key concept in modern education to get away with, so I set about finding out what it is.

I begged the help of an exceptionally bright deputy head on it.

'David. Is it just increased use of peer assessment?'

'No. It's more complicated than that.'

'Is it increased self-assessment?'

'No. It's more complicated even than that.'

Having looked at the Qualifications and Curriculum Authority site, I've still not found out what it is. Assessment for learning has ten principles, none of which I have even the most cursory understanding of! Apparently, assessment for learning 'should be part of effective planning of teaching and learning', 'should focus on how students learn' and 'should be recognised as central to classroom practice'.

I rarely plan lessons with anything more than four lines in a planner, don't know how children learn and can't include it in my practice because I don't know what it is. And none of these principles are getting anywhere near telling me.

To get away from the grandly expressed, empty waffle, I've gone to the source. It seems that the notion of AfL comes from a research document written by Dylan Wiliam and Paul Black, *Inside the Black Box: Raising Standards through Classroom Assessment*.

I've witnessed Wiliam speak. He has profoundly serious and sensible things to say about education. It is a further document though – the Assessment Reform Group's pamphlet *Assessment for Learning: Beyond the Black Box* – that appears to be the bridge between the research and its implementation in schools. These 12 slim pages start with the proclamation that Wiliam and Black's initial research has 'proved without a shadow of a doubt that, when carried out effectively, informal classroom assessment with constructive feedback to the student will raise levels of attainment', and goes on to state that: 'Although it is now fairly widely accepted that this form of assessment and feedback is important, the development of practice in this area will need a concerted policy-making push.'

There doesn't appear to be too much to argue with there, though Wiliam and Black identify an 'informal' process, and the authors of *Assessment for Learning* seem intent on formalising it. And so the next 11 pages come up with ideas about what assessment for learning will look like.

And you know what, my deputy head was right. It is more complicated even than increased use of peer assessment and self-assessment. Assessment for learning, which has been presented to teachers as some kind of complex grail, is increased use of peer assessment, self-assessment and of teacher assessment.

Wiliam spoke recently on Teachers' TV about his hopes for an improved synthesis between research and practice.

This is eminently sensible. However, it seems that in the ten years it has taken for the ideas from *Inside the Black Box* to filter down into practice, it has lost a lot in translation. My experience of assessment for learning has been having to attempt to decode a load of opaque gruel that refuses to give up its meaning; followed by a fairly certain realisation that observed lessons that do not have some form of peer or self-assessment are now judged to be somehow dysfunctional.

As a teacher, I would love to have a better relationship with research, and to have time to devote to that relationship. But when the practitioners at the teacher end of it are handed the information after it has been rendered near meaningless by a series of sieves over many years, and that information is presented to us as yet another top-down dictate that the acceptable, state approved version of teaching has altered slightly, then that day looks a long way off.

Satisfactory?

Working with a group of English teachers on the south coast a couple of weeks ago, I committed the INSET provider's greatest sin. I ran out of material. Following a couple of fidgety minutes, twitching, umming and erring, I improvised (quite brilliantly I thought) and decided we should, well, kind of, like, have a chat. And so, a part of an INSET provision that was meant to be providing teachers with strategies for improving GCSE results took the form of a group therapy session.

One young teacher shared her experience of the most recent lesson observation she'd had, and in which she had been judged to be 'satisfactory'. 'Hi,' she said, 'I'm Jill and I'm – and I don't know how to say this really – I'm a "satisfactory" teacher. It's really hit me,' her voice trembling with emotion. 'I don't think I'm satisfactory. But until the next lesson observation, I'm carrying this burden of doubt around. All day. Every day.' Her colleagues all jumped in to reassure her that she wasn't, in any way, anywhere near being 'satisfactory', and that the observers had got it all wrong. And I thought ...

What a surreal profession! A profession in which a judgement that, in any sane world, would be taken to mean 'giving satisfaction', actually causes the recipient of that judgement to lapse into a state of depression. Imagine a bank clerk, for instance, who has been told that their performance has been satisfactory and that they have qualified for their yearly pay rise (including enhanced pension rights). Do they spend the following months in an inferno of self-doubt? Do they 'eck as like. Straight after receiving it, they cartwheel out of the office, a tangle of feverishly joyful limbs, straight in the direction of the nearest publicly licensed retailer of champagne and oysters.

So why do we, as teachers, take the judgement of satisfactory as a condemnation? The answer is in the punctuation. Because 'satisfactory' in inverted commas in no way means the same thing as satisfactory without them. If an observer were observing a genuinely satisfactory (without inverted commas) lesson, they'd be liable to leave it, unable to stop themselves from expressing their gratitude to the teacher. 'My God, young lady. What a satisfactory lesson! I don't think I'll be able to sit in the back of another one until tomorrow, for, in truth, I am replete of learning.' They may even choose, when the occasion demands, to let out a subtle belch of professional gratitude.

But they don't. Because 'satisfactory' when applied to schools and lessons is shorthand for, 'Well, it'll do, but, let's face it: you're a bit shit really.'

What can we conclude from this? That the fast-moving world of education (note, lack of inverted commas) is too often the victim of linguistic weaselry. Call a school a new name, and *voila*, it's a better school. Call a school 'specialist', and *voici*, you have genuine specialism. Rename a process 'learning and teaching' and immediately teachers become ego-free facilitators. Speak enough about 'personalisation' (note, inverted commas), and someone, in some school, somewhere, surely, will make a brave, though futile and doomed, attempt to write 30 different lesson plans for each lesson; before keeling over with a combined heart attack and nervous breakdown in the second week of September.

When I first started sitting in the back of other teachers' lessons pretending that I was capable of doing all the things in a single lesson that I was judging them on, the judgement would be to allocate one of seven grades. These went from 'excellent', through 'very good' and 'good', into the direction of 'satisfactory' and its spindlier brother 'unsatisfactory', from thence into the dark realms of 'poor' and 'very poor'.

No more. What should we have read into the change from this to the bald four grades currently in use, where lessons are either 'outstanding', 'good', 'satisfactory' or 'inadequate'? We conclude that 'excellence' is no longer enough. 'Good' is a broad church indeed. 'Satisfactory' means little better than the level beneath it. And you can't dip your toes into 'unsatisfactory' any more; get that particular digit wet and you are immediately and summarily deemed 'inadequate'.

Why did OFSTED change the number of grades, and in so doing minimise both the lesson observer's palette and the level of nuance they could apply to their judgement? One could form a theory that it is to make it easier to get rid of teachers judged as underperforming, and to broaden this notional group of teachers as a cohort. In dispensing with 'unsatisfactory', 'poor' and 'very poor', replacing them with the full facial tattoo of 'inadequate', they have made judgement at the lower end binary.

There are no degrees of 'unsatisfactory' performance any more, just pass and fail. Where, prior to this narrowing (which I believe is referred to in OFSTED circles as 'rigour'), management teams might be able to look at the data and differentiate between those teachers who'd just had an off lesson and those who may want to consider alternative employment, these two groups of teachers are now lumped together in special measures.

The further impact is that terming the lower level the unarguably and terminally emphatic 'inadequate', rather than the less pejorative and more temporary sounding 'unsatisfactory', it causes inspectors, who are human after all, a moment's hesitation before they dispense a number; the ultimate impact of which might be a professional taking the long walk of shame down to the labour exchange. This will mean that many teachers who receive a 'satisfactory' judgement under the current regime would, under the previous grading system, have been judged 'unsatisfactory'.

And so my young friend on the south coast is right to be worried by being judged 'satisfactory'. In the distorting, surrealist mirrors of our industry 'satisfactory', in fact, means quite the opposite.

ICT

By way of an introduction, here is a series of articles I had laughingly entitled (to myself – no one else knew of this, until the last one) the 'Wind Up a Spod' series. They achieved their intent, making a number of people who very much enjoy spending time with their computers a bit grumpy; and as a result, I still get the odd invitation to ICT conferences where I am aware I am being invited simply so they can throw potatoes at me. I'm not much fond of potatoes, so don't bother turning up.

Wind Up a Spod 1

I am sick, sick, sick to death of PowerPoint, and sick of sitting at INSET days being shown a set of slides with bullet points and having them read to me very ... very ... slowly. 'Look,' my inner voice shouts, 'I am a graduate professional. I can read. Give me the handouts and I'll have them digested in two minutes. It shouldn't take the whole school staff two hours in an inferno of boredom for you to make three salient points.'

PowerPoint, as Ian Gilbert memorably puts it, is merely an 'overhead projector on steroids'. And this is the problem with much of the use of ICT in schools: we are all so busy showing off the fact that we can now button our new waistcoat that nobody has had the guts to point out that it is see-through.

A journalist suggested recently that there are digital natives (who've grown up fluent in a world in which ICT is ubiquitous) and digital immigrants (spitting at a much distrusted mobile phone which fails to obey their commands). Well, there's a further group of us trapped in some digital hinterland, giving a veneer of competence that's enough to fool your Grandad, but which any 20-year-old would be able to put their finger straight through in an instant.

Brenda Despontin, president of the Girls' Schools Association, has asked: 'Where is the serious debate on the desirability of so much technology?'

The use of ICT in schools is surely worthy of a debate in which teachers actually get a say, and from which those companies selling the equipment are excluded.

ICT has been presented to the education community as a panacea, and if you are not using it to its full capacity you are left feeling the aged inadequate shaking their leg epileptically to a ragga tune.

I am still stuck in that hinterland where I think ICT in schools is a great idea (and all that), but am still rendered shamefaced while caught in stock cupboards sniffing books with lascivious intent. The problem with ICT as a panacea, apart from the fact that the stuff it is replacing – books, human contact and language – was so well designed in the first place, is that it's been thrown at us with neither instruction manual nor time to read one if one existed.

As a result, much of ICT use in schools is piss poor, squared. All of us have witnessed some 'imported for a twilight session' ICT whizz make the interactive whiteboard sing, clap its hands and perform a pelvis-breaking dance. A select few of us, however, will have translated that training into a single trick. A trick we desperately hope will fox OFSTED into believing that we are anything other than pasty incompetents wearing a none-too-convincing ICT-wizard mask.

Some of the most regular users of ICT in British schools are often using it to hide the fact that they are, in fact, the most depleted of the many tired faces in a staffroom. If you want to get away with it, then there is no surer way than plugging your unruly brood into the brave new world of technology, and taking a well earned rest. You can watch blithely on as they dial up chatrooms, in which they may well receive a radically different curriculum from other adults with radically different experiences of institutional life.

Much of ICT use in schools consists of the 'plug 'em in, shut 'em up, get to the end of the lesson' mantra, and I wonder if it is the fact that children are quiet and controlled while tranquilised by this modern day soma that it has been sold to us as a cure-all for the problems of male under-attainment. 'They must be learning. They're quiet, aren't they?'

I would argue that boys – who are supposedly meant to learn more from ICT lessons than through any other form of instruction – may well be better off spending a lesson writing one full sentence with a pencil than they are tapping out one word every 20 minutes on a PC.

This is not to say there aren't fantastically imaginative practitioners working with computers who have come up with innovative ways of learning. Stephen Heppell, for instance, is seen as a visionary by many. It is just that bog-standard professionals get little or no time whatsoever to investigate these. To provide exciting learning experiences with new software requires time for teachers to learn how to use it. To learn how to use it you need time to experiment, to play. And there is not much in the way of playtime available for mainscale teachers in British schools.

Consequently, the interactive whiteboard is used in many secondary schools to display lesson objectives, show movies at the end of term and very little else. It may well be a fantastic tool, but many of us, mainly those in secondary schools, don't have the first idea how to work the bloody thing!

I used to have a record collection until big business dictated I buy the albums all over again on the new, more efficient format, the CD. I am now told I must once again buy songs I already own, this time for my iPod. Given the software companies' skills at selling us the useless, it is difficult to dispense with the suspicion that schools packed with computers are, to an extent, the government caving in to the pressures of powerful corporations. Which is enough to send me running back to the stock cupboard armed with my trusty pencil for yet another guilty sniff of a book. A book which will, in all probability, have been written with a feather ripped from a duck's bum.

Wind Up a Spod 2

There's a fantastic, though sadly apocryphal, story about the early days of the space race. NASA, so it goes, spent billions of dollars and years of research creating the world's first zero gravity ballpoint. The pen was a success, eventually retrieving some of its mammoth development costs by becoming a hit with schoolboy nerds, finding its way into many a speccy American's Christmas stocking. Given the same problem, the Russians came up with a more elegant solution: they used a pencil.

And it is the relationship between nerds and pencils with which the column is concerned this month. An ill wind blew me onto a train going to Earls Court recently, the same day as the rank masses of software salesmen gathered at the British Educational Training and Technology (BETT) Show. A further gust took me into the main building of Olympia where, wandering without aim about the vast spaces, colourful displays and keening avarice, a thought struck me. Ambling around BETT, I wondered whether a better, more symbolically useful display would be to situate a single glass case in the middle of the cavernous Grand Hall, in which is displayed a single 2H pencil.

The sad and unpublicised fact is that most of the wares for sale at BETT are of spurious educational benefit, and I wonder why there aren't more teachers prepared to don their 'lone voice in the wilderness cloaks' and take a stand here against the pernicious, creeping rise of these dumb tools and their bovine, unmalleable functionality.

Perhaps the reason is that to do so is to put oneself up against a moneyed and mouthy enemy. The ICT evangelists defend the utility on which their careers and burgeoning influence are based with admirable verve. But they would wouldn't they? Not only is this multi-million pound industry their lifeblood, but it is its own marketing tool: ICT has given the, till now mercifully silent, blogger a new sense of the power of his own voice, and you can bet he is not afraid to step out of the shadows, stick a new piece of Sellotape to his glasses and declare his power.

The result is that in government circles, ICT is now entirely analogous with creativity. One cannot credibly make any claim to being a creative teacher without a fistful of palmtop devices ruining the line of your back trouser pocket. This is entirely stupid. Real creativity is caused by working within constraints. A truly creative teacher is one who can enter a classroom with only a marker pen for company and produce a brilliant lesson using only their professional brilliance and a stern expression.

I have worked in six schools, and with the exception of one teacher, Kevin Ducker, I have not seen much use of ICT that did anything much more than give very poor teachers an easy lesson behaviourally. The interactive whiteboards that were meant to radicalise our teaching have been proven to make no real difference, other than encouraging the kind of didactic, front of class teaching that is supposed to induce the least learning in our charges. The computerised voting systems that were sold to us as revolutionising lessons are now gathering dust in a cupboard, having been used three times, before being replaced by a return to the more efficient show of hands.

One particular award-winning package exemplifies the problem here: the celebrated marketing video which asks children to recreate an Andy Warhol print on the computer, briefly acknowledging that Warhol 'did it using screen-printing'. In which case, why not teach the children how to do it the way Warhol did it? One cannot sit through many minutes of this without wondering what is desperately wrong with teaching kids to paint using (and I know this comes across as sheer madness), erm, paint.

Using a computer to replicate the brushstrokes of, for instance, the Impressionists, is a one-sided equation which ignores much of the artists' methodology. The Impressionists, like all artists, were as much about input as they were about style, and perceived it as vital that they took in the sensory input of fresh air to be able to paint. It is not possible to properly replicate the experience of being an Impressionist painter either in the simulacrum brushstrokes of the paint facility, or in the arid environment of the ICT classroom.

And it is this arse-about-face aspect of ICT provision that so enrages. Virtuality is not the real thing. It is the responsibility of education to enrich children's experience of the world, and of life; and ICT's hidden agenda, the message of which is that everything nature produces can be better fabricated, may have made for an interesting thesis in 19th-century France, but does not hold any water at all now we are in possession of the revolution. An inspiring education is a sensory joy and the idiotic pre-eminence of the computer is a denial of this.

Why then has the budget been placed into the hands of the nerds? Because there is an agenda here. BECTA's strategic objectives include 'to save the education system £100 million over three years'. How are they going to achieve this? Given that all the software packages are made by the private industry the government is so keen to involve in schools, and these are driven by a motive for profit, their wares are far from free. How then are we to spend to save? I think you already know the answer. A further of BECTA's objectives is to 'double the numbers of teachers using technology to support personalisation'. These two objectives are linked. The idea being that if a computer can be used to personalise education, then there will eventually be no need for learning support in human form.

The further agenda is also economic. If we are working towards a 'knowledge economy', in foregrounding ICT use above any other skill, we are promoting an economy in which only one form of knowledge is perceived as viable or useful; and a lesson wasted on a clumsy, two-sentence PowerPoint presentation is of more value than reading a book.

The personalisation agenda has always been about sliding in whatever policy feint found its way onto a beer mat after a Whitehall lunch, but combine this with the unquestioned flooding of schools with useless IT solutions to problems that didn't exist and, in five years' time, you've got Robbie the Robot running the special needs department and difficult-to-teach kids excluded from school altogether, as their learning can be better personalised at home. I used to be for progress. But it went too far.

Wind Up a Spod 3 – The Interactive Whiteboard

Back in the old days, a monstrous, notionally portable behemoth sat centre stage in classrooms across the land: the blackboard. A coiled sheet of continuous canvas, painted black, drawn across two parallel rollers and mounted on a sturdy oak frame; they were black holes of attention, sucking the lives out of children and teachers alike.

It had its uses, the blackboard, though these were limited. An imaginative science teacher might get up a head of steam and pull down violently on one of its metal runners to demonstrate friction, and many is the teacher who, faced with an unruly class, would threaten the ultimate sanction: scratching their nails down it.

But it came with issues. Not only was it difficult to write in any legible manner on it, but the fact that you had to do so in chalk made a teacher's lot an intolerable circle of purgatory. Younger teachers will never have had to endure the repugnant, repetitive limbo of writing with pieces of white rock. It got all over your favourite trousers, right into your pores and all the way up your nose. Anyone practised in manual labour will be well aware that one of the less public and least appealing facets of an honest day's toil is the black deposits you have to extract from your nose at the end of the day. The blackboard teacher would have similar problems with claggier, whiter versions of the same. What is more, a teacher unused to astringent and moisturiser (as many of us were in those far distant days), would have to get used to the dull and pallid skin tone that chalk dust would leave on any pedagogue's permanently pale puss.

The fact that chalk dust embedded itself into the skin also allowed teachers to coin a singularly ridiculous metaphor with which to describe their working lives: teachers didn't work in schools, no, they toiled at the 'chalkface'. A lot of male teachers spend their lives in fear of their job being seen for the fundamentally poncey pass-time it is, and coining a term that compared reading a lovely story to a classroom full of 4-year-olds to the environment endured by our comrades in toil, the miners, somehow masculinised our work. We were deluded. The fact that we had cause to invent such a ludicrously self-pitying metaphor served only to confirm all the more, and for good, that we are fundamentally poncey.

And we cried poncey tears of blessed relief when the blackboard was cast out upon the bonfire of progress, to be replaced by its more handsome cousin: the whiteboard. The whiteboard was newer, stronger, fitter for purpose. We fell so headlong into its seductive clutches we could even forgive, or ignore, the uncomfortable hints of eugenicism in its nomenclature: black bad, white better. And for two or three years we would waltz in a carefree manner in front of the whiteboard delighting in the new freedoms it gave us.

No longer were we chained by the classroom's central device. It was possible to do so many things easily with the whiteboard that the blackboard had denied us. They were so vast we could write to the end of the line; they lent themselves to colour, so we could draw convincing maps or fairy castles; and crucially, readers of *Education Guardian*, crucially, you could illustrate thought on them in real time. I repeat. You. Could. Illustrate. Thought. In. Real. Time.

You can't illustrate thought in real time any more. For the whiteboard too has been thrown on that very same fire on which flicker the embers of its dead cousin. Every head teacher showing prospective parents around the school will proudly announce that each classroom has an interactive smart-board. These now stand as the new behemoths of progress at the centre of the room, the whiteboard reduced in size, or shifted to a fusty corner; sometimes even split in two, so that two useless, half-sized mini-versions now flank their nemesis, looking on apologetically and enviously as the projector buzzes. (Or, as is often the case, doesn't.)

Like the blackboard before them, the smart-board has its uses, though they are more limited than any head teacher would have you believe. They are great for showing photos, bringing a visual stimulus into lessons and they show a mean DVD. But their place at the front of the class means that every lesson must now have a PowerPoint presentation and a teacher's key tool nowadays is the memory stick on which they keep these. The smart-board's central positioning destroys a teacher's ability to be spontaneous. You cannot come in any more with a couple of board markers and a handful of good ideas – the blind object at the room's focal point mocks you too heartily if you do so. 'Why have you not turned me on?' it screams. 'Why have you not sat up all evening downloading pictures that would make me look as if I had some vital use? You are lazy and should be sacked.'

Alexandre Borovik, a Professor of Pure Maths at Manchester University, who remains loyal to the blackboard, has a good many opinions about 'the snake oil peddlers from Staff Development and Teaching Quality who cannot imagine an "Enhanced learning environment" without an all-singing, all-dancing PowerPoint presentation'.

He speaks as a blackboard mathematician, but his points resonate with this whiteboard English teacher: 'A mathematics teacher is not just conveying information, he or she teaches to think mathematically, and teaches by example, in real time. It is crucially important to be in full control of timing and tempo of the narrative. If a lecture involves calculations, it is crucially important to let students feel the subtle play of rhythms, emphasise switches and branch points in the procedure, highlight recursion and reduction to simpler cases.'

This rings Notre Dame-sized bells with me. If I am modelling sentence construction or the semicolon, drawing a map illustrating colonialism in Africa or scribing rude arrows outlining connections between seemingly disparate ideas, I want to be able to do it quickly; as quick as I think; as quick as I talk. I want to be able to teach with my whole body, use gesture, employ pause to illustrate nuance, become as one with the board; becoming, in those rare moments of flow, both dancer and dance. I cannot do this any more, because the board in the centre of the room dictates that, rather than pirouette, twist and enthuse, I click a frigid button instead. They have their uses smart-boards, but their position in the centre gives them an undeserved primacy. If you have any say in where yours goes, get them to put it at the side of the room. If you don't, try asking for it to be given to someone more worthy than you; and you'll make do with your old whiteboard.

Failed Attempt at Wind Up a Spod 4

I signed up to bury Twitter. Not to praise it. To complete the last part of a series of columns I had entitled the 'Wind Up a Spod' series, with which I would deliberately elicit further spluttering outrage from the educators who spend much of their lives chuffed to the goolies whilst ogling Google, blogging about its noodle-boggling goodness.

My first – and I still feel ever so slightly bilious using this word (as it makes me feel like an uncle dancing at a wedding to the happy, teenage couple's favourite grime track) – 'tweets' were brief exercises designed to satirise the somewhat ridiculous narcissism I perceived in the Twitter user. Who on earth could be so assured of their own importance that they would think their 140 character dribbles would be of any interest to anyone with anything corresponding to a life?

And so, my first utterances included on the 25th June, 'Realising I can't spell pheasant,' to be followed four days later by, 'Worrying about kidneys (mine)' and, from then, on to the all-time classic, 'Pondering the phrase "Big Jessie".'

It continued in this vein until such point as absent-mindedly scribing the none more inconsequential line, 'Failing to be amusing on the subject of boys' achievement on a Saturday night. Work/life balance. I've heard of it.' Current UK Secondary Teacher of the Year, David Miller, on recognising a soul in partial torment working too hard on a Saturday night and missing *Match of the Day*, used Twitter to reach all the way across from Lower Dumbarton and, with it, dispensed a much needed, though thankfully virtual, empathetic cuddle. Cuddles, they melt cynicism. And at that very moment my feelings about Twitter changed. If it is a piece of functionality that can cause the casually wept lonely tear to reach the ears of a concerned peer then, in an education system that seems less and less to recognise or care about teachers' humanity, it is a form of social networking that allows one to access the kind word, the piece of professional advice, perhaps even the readily located resource.

Twitter devotee Laura Doggett, Director of E-learning at Westfield Community Technology College, has written an article (available at www.lauradoggett.com), which is held to be seminal by those inclined to witter about Twitter. In 'Nine Reasons Teachers Should Use Twitter' she lists, erm, nine reasons that it is a useful tool for professional development. Not the least of these is that, as a medium, it is instantaneous. You can ask a question from your network of newly minted professional allies and receive a reply almost instantly. The question could be about where to find a resource on a specific subject, or whether anyone has advice about how to deal with a difficult work situation, and it is likely it will receive a series of pithy yet considered answers within the hour from various sources.

Laura also refers to the fact that Twitter gives access to experts both local and global. You have the option of following people you might see face to face, day to day or otherwise, or to follow globally recognised experts, who, given that it only costs them a minute to reply and there is no implication that they will get into an onerous, protracted correspondence if they do so, will actually reply if you ask them a question. As an example, following American educationist and former teacher, Alfie Kohn, has given me access to a series of articles that I would not otherwise have encountered; specifically one about the results of the famous marshmallow test that calls into question one of the central tenets of the burgeoning emotional intelligence industry.

Furthermore, having access to a ready network of peers means that not only do you have the ability to run ideas by people, get them peer reviewed so to speak but, as Laura points out, Twitter causes the blank canvas to be potentially opaque. If working on, for instance, a scheme of work or an observed lesson, you can ask for and get immediate feedback as to where the best work has been done on this subject. All it takes is a cry for help, and such is the all-pervasive sense of fraternity on Twitter that you get a guiding hand on your shoulder within seconds of asking for it.

As a time commitment getting something out of Twitter comes with negligible cost, and its potential benefits in terms of intellectual grazing away from the specific fenced enclave of those who earn their corn from the education racket are manifold. Amongst the education bodies and professionals I follow, I also tune into the wisdoms of the two greatest songwriters of the late 20th and early 21st century: Cathal Coughlan and Mark Eitzel. Sadly, being wise, they have better things to do than sit in front of a screen three quarters of their waking life recording every banal detail of their existence. But, y'know … as an idea, briefly engaging with the philosophical musings of the great on a day-to-day basis has value. As one twitterer puts it: 'Following smart people on Twitter is like a mental shot of espresso.' And if you have sufficient imagination to locate heroes less parochially obvious than Stephen Fry or less odious than Jonathan Ross, then there is every possibility that just logging on would lead to a rewarding, transient engagement with a great mind.

Last year I was quoted in another newspaper questioning the use of Twitter in classrooms: 'There should be more thought and research into whether we really want to be promoting in schools a means of social networking that limits the amount of characters one can use. Using Twitter to teach children all that communication must, by definition, lack depth of any sort, and is plainly mad.' I have revised my opinion. It is the brevity of Twitter that makes it potentially enormously useful in the classroom. Were it not on the list of sites banned by the network manager we might be able to use it to teach children how to write with elegance and simplicity. We might even, if we were imaginative, get students to write a series of haikus in a lesson that they can then publish immediately. We might. But, generally speaking, we don't have the equipment for the 21st-century classroom, and where we do, it is usually broken.

People and Personalities

What's So Wrong With Liking Your Students?

Sometime in 1998 a rock journalist wrote that my face was 'like a saddlebag that's been dragged over ten miles of scrub'. He went on to describe the physiological effects of laughter on it: 'His skin wrinkles up around his eyes until it looks like the contour map of a particularly steep mountain.' I have spent a lot of money on expensive moisturiser in the last eight years. It doesn't work.

He also went on to say nice things about the record I had made, but these passed almost unnoticed. The point is, we don't even register the nice things people say about us, but the nasty ones stick.

If you put your face up to be kissed you are, of course, going to get it royally slapped; but nothing could ever have prepared me for the vitriol that came my way six months ago from the visitors to a website run for teachers. Their reaction to my teaching/demeanour in a daft telly programme fair took my breath away. Safely nestled 'neath pseudonyms such as 'Celebrity Gossip Fan' some of the more embittered members of the teaching profession took it in turns to launch into an astonishingly colourful array of character assassinations. In amongst the critiques of my accent and accusations of being a manic-depressive, one particular gripe loomed large: I was too friendly with my charges.

One of this shrieking chorus, a gentleman by the pseudonym of 'Freddie 92' referred to the 'David Brent/Phil

Beadle type who longs to be accepted by teenagers who, in a few years time, will join the rest of us laughing at them.' 'Salsera', in a tone of near hysteric exasperation exclaimed, 'We are not supposed to be bezzie mates with the students – we are teachers.'

Lest I be accused of using the pages of a newspaper for a personal catharsis, (or of conducting a childish vendetta) let me just stamp my cotton booty, throw my rattle and scream it isn't fair! My 'bezzie' mate is an EAL (English as an additional language) teacher from Widnes. And besides that, Freddie 92 knows nothing of what I long for. And besides even that, if he did know he'd probably have me arrested.

Seriously though, for all their swingeing lack of generosity of spirit, these visitors to web chat forums raise an interesting point: is there a correct way of running a professional relationship with the children you teach? Can you be too friendly?

A head teacher, under whom I once served, was quite a fan of the notion of 'gravitas'. Whilst administering a sound telling off to his professionally trained, graduate staff, he would propound the merits of a starched back and an unforgiving approach. His approach was partially successful. He ran a tight ship: everyone was so petrified of his lack of any apparent humanity they'd do absolutely anything he said.

But I don't much like fear. I don't like being made to feel it myself and I don't like inspiring it in others. It is an untrustworthy motivator since it breeds resentment and ignites the desire for revenge. Any teacher can instantaneously obtain gravitas in the eyes of their students by manifesting a passion for their subject.

Those who advocate the merits of a distant, disinterested professionalism would argue that it is all about expectations: children will rise to whatever expectations are set for them. I agree. Be polite to your students and it is reasonable for you to expect that they act in kind. Display good manners and you will receive them. Give trust and you get it back. Ever wondered why so many children loved primary school and flourished at it, only to find their secondary school education stifling and scary? Go by your local primary at 9 a.m. and observe the relationships between small children and their teachers.

There is a slandering implication on teachers who attempt to relate to their students as human beings that they are somehow making up for deficiencies in their own lives. You could see this another way: the teacher who knows the value of love from their own life will be keen to pass its credo on to others. Of course, there is a chalk line that cannot be crossed, but this line is there, again, to make the students feel safe and secure. It is decidedly not there so some pocket despot can act out their own Hitler fantasies.

Sadly, my colleagues on the world wide web somewhat undermined their argument by going a bit too far. One wanted to see 'How much of that [disruptive] behaviour would persist if it were met with a caning every time it appeared.' While 'Liam G' suggested one of the pupils on the programme be, 'Made to stay minus his toothbrush, pillow, given some ****e clothes, maybe shaved his head. (with **** wrote in his hair).' I have left Liam G's punctuation to speak for itself. And no, I have no idea what the expletives are.

I am of the fervent belief that if there is a secret to teaching well it is this: you must like the children you teach and be able to show them you do. It is the key to a vocation. I don't think the person who proposed they 'dump these 16 kids in the middle of the African desert' is in the right profession. Professionalism and being friendly are not mutually exclusive; and proper respect from students is obtained not through pomp or from detention, but from awarding children human dignity and demonstrating your own respect of it.

Edutainment

It is likely that Christine Gilbert's[10] pronouncement will cause a certain buzzing of the irate on teachers' noticeboards: 'If I'd wanted to be a performing monkey I would have joined the circus.' Some members of the teaching profession feel that anyone who has the temerity to point out the causal link between being bored and behaving poorly is actually launching into a concerted attack on the standards of teaching in the country. But Gilbert is right to draw this link.

In many of the schools that serve poorer areas, with students' attention spans decimated by a diet of sugary snacks, video games and 20 channels of fast-edited crud on the cathode ray tube, student engagement is not just an issue; it is the issue. The teacher who is not able to induce open mouths expressing both 'awe' and 'wonder' in their charges within the first ten minutes of a lesson is likely to witness the jaws of those mouths slacken as one, as behaviour heads quickly in the direction of 'off-task'.

---

[10] This was written in response to the head of OFSTED claiming that boring lessons cause poor behaviour.

This puts teachers at the sharp end under irrefutable pressure to entertain. Losing a difficult class in the first ten minutes of a double lesson on Friday afternoon presents the poor teacher with a two-hour inferno of self-doubt, shouting, tearing their hair out, perhaps even walking out.

Consequently, many teachers choose to develop a style of classroom management too easily satirised by some sections of the education community as being 'edutainment'. Edutainment is merely the boring teacher's shorthand for good practice. The 'edutainer' will use a variety of stimuli, recognise that children learn best when they talk to each other in groups and will employ the arts as a key part of their methodology.

Whilst there are some classes so engrained in routines of awful behaviour that all the bells and whistles in the world won't reach them, in general, kids really only mess about when they are bored. Gilbert is merely drawing teachers' attention to the simplest answer to the difficult class. Don't bore them.

Most teachers understand this without having to be told. However, my own experience has been predominantly in the inner city, and avoiding student boredom in these environments is a prerequisite for teachers' survival. There is a world outside of the crucibles; and it may be that, in schools where children don't dismantle the furniture if a teacher talks at them for two hours, didactic styles of instruction are more prevalent.

However, as Ms Gilbert is no doubt aware, planning exciting lessons is a time-consuming activity. Vast swathes of a teacher's time in an over-regulated education system is spent proving they are doing the job, rather than actually doing it. If Ms Gilbert wants more 'buzzy' lessons, perhaps the focus should be less on top-down dictates, than in reducing teacher workload, so that we have the time to engage, to excite and, yes, even to entertain.

Haircuts

I spent the last holiday watching the leaves fall in Northern Holland and bingeing on that most cuddly of literary genres, the teacher memoir. At one point I was up to one a day, and have had to make a concerted effort to cut down ever since.

Over the space of the week I reread both of Francis Gilbert's volumes, tucked into Frank McCourt's overly loquacious *Teacher Man*, rambled through Oenone Crossley-Holland's *Hands Up*, cried with convulsive laughter at Frank Chalk's *It's Your Time You're Wasting: A Teacher's Tales of Classroom Hell* and shed sadder tears at Ian Whitwham's *At the Chalkface: Great Moments in Education*. And it is the last of these that has prompted the subject of this column: students' errant barnets. There is a section in this profoundly human and inspiring book entitled, 'Seth in the Sixth Form'. I have now read it seven times. It pricks the ducts.

In it Whitwham, an inner city English teacher for over 30 years, and therefore a supremely qualified cataloguer of educational change, describes the effects of the growing pressures of conformity on a member of his sixth form class, Seth.

Seth belongs to 'that fine English tradition of languid bohemians ... daft hair and grim pallor and skinny cryptic T-shirts'. Whitwham recognises elements of his own younger self in Seth: a younger self who went to Dylan gigs, read (and dressed like) Kerouac and churned out reams of bad verse that his English teacher indulged. There is the sadness of a well full of souls in Whitwham's words as he notes that it was easier to be bohemian in those days: 'These days the sixth form is all about modules and targets and uniforms.'

His wistful conclusion is where the waterworks hit: 'Jarvis wears kohl and skull earrings and Rhapsody has gone all left bank and discovered Francoise Hardy. They're bright and funny – and seventeen. A delight. The best. If we continue to treat them like this, we will lose them.'

It rings a particular bell, as I have taught a couple of Seth's last year and this: one female, one male. Hannah, last year, remarking on a singularly poorly achieved red silk suit I can no longer get away with, remarked wrongly that I was the only teacher in the school who put any real effort into what I wore. She delighted me in doing so, as Hannah herself clearly put a lot of effort into her appearance: hair always an interesting colour, nose stud just so, school uniform creatively customised. In conversation about her, another teacher spoke somewhat witheringly of the parenting she'd received. 'They think it's important that she expresses herself!' said Mr Teacher, a barely concealed sneer palpating across his moustache.

Rob, who is in one of the two year eleven classes I am teaching this year, dyes his hair too. It is an unnatural boot polish black, extravagantly styled, feathered into the inversion of a quiff so that it covers half of his face. He looks great, but in no way straight. Thankfully, the school does not think it would be a good idea to take his natural sense of cool, his rebel spirit, his sense of himself as being a unique soul, and deem it unsuitable; and so he crouches over his exercise book, creating another love poem for his girlfriend, his fringe tickling the paper.

My sadness is that in many schools Rob would not be allowed to decide what he does with his hair, which, lest you need reminding, is part of him. Uniform policy is increasingly taking an absurdly draconian shift in its approach to the decisions kids make about how they wear their hair, banning any style more interesting than that you would ordinarily find on an Abbey National correspondence clerk clad in a Next business suit. Uniform policies nowadays are uniformly filled with such pitifully and vehemently ignorant statements, as 'Patterns cut into the hair are not acceptable.' Not acceptable to whom? Or, 'Hair colour will be restricted to that found in normal hair.' And normal means, exactly? A setting on a washing machine.

This risible zero tolerance to self-expression policy is increasingly the norm. One school policy promises a punishment as imaginative as anything Tomás de Torquemada might have designed. 'Students wearing unacceptable hairstyles should be sent to the Head of Year, who will arrange for them to be kept out of lessons until the hairstyle has grown out.' Given that it can take a year or two for hair dye to grow out, one can imagine a room full of lonely, educationally malnourished children, sitting ennui-ridden for months on end with little else to do other than willing their hair to grow faster.

Some of these rules are also, by definition, racist. As Gladston Priestley, 13, a student at Hutton CE Grammar School found out when he had his hair put into a cornrow. He was put into isolation, until such time as he took them out. Gladston's mum, Mary Tremlett, hit the nail on the head in response: 'It's part of his culture ... I want the school to reconsider his hair. I'm not prepared to have my son in isolation.'

Schools outlawing steps being cut into the hair, shaved shapes or braiding, do so not only with a deeply flawed sense of both aesthetics and equalities issues, but directly against the government's guidance on the same. The DCSF guidance to schools on school uniform and related policies states: 'An example of indirect discrimination could be a school that bans "cornrow" hairstyles. As these are more likely to be adopted by specific racial groups, banning this type of hairstyle without justification could constitute indirect racial discrimination.' For 'could' read, this has not been tested yet in law, but we suspect such discrimination would be found to be illegal, so don't push it too far with the fascism.

Some school leaders' petty insistence on inflicting their own lack of anything resembling panache or style onto people who are experimenting with versions of who they might be smacks, to me, of horrific jealousy of youth. Should we really be interested in seeing self-expression as punishable non-conformity? If we continue to treat them like this we will surely lose them.

Neckties

Curse the Croatian mercenary who, during the Thirty Years War, first brought the fabric torture device (the necktie) to the attention of the French; who, in turn, thought it so ooh-la-la, they adopted the cravat as a key part of daywear. Curse too those bleedin' macaronis. Bloody tourists, who brought the fashion to these shores after their grand tours abroad. And finally, double curse the swines who promote the wearing of a piece of cloth around the neck – which is the shape of a noose and has no discernible function – as being a sign of status and respectability.

I've always detested being forced to wear a tie. They are uncomfortable, always thinner (or fatter) than you want them to be and seem to serve the sole function of making explicit one caste's dominance over the other.

Any senior manager in a British school will tell you that uniform is half the battle: take a fairly draconian stance on this, and many of the worst behavioural infractions don't occur. Take a tough line on the wearing of trainers, and there will be fewer murders. It works. But with the ever-vaporous notion of ethos the order of the decade, we have a new order of schools for which the insistence on children wearing a knotted piece of striped polyester around their necks constitutes the visual confirmation of ethos's presence.

The necktie is undergoing a resurgence in some institutions; a result, in part, of the government's desire for the state system to import the DNA of the independent sector. Make a schoolboy from a Bermondsey council estate, who has grown up with neither male role model nor antecedents with any respect for education, dress in the manner of a student from a private school in Tring, and they are, magically, the same animal.

The issue is, if you give savvy students a compulsory stricture that is so absurd it cries out to be subverted, they will start getting busy with the subversion.

There are three main flavours of rebellion with which the pleasingly seditious schoolchild will obey the letter of the rule whilst rejecting the spirit. The most thuggishly obvious of these is the 'who ate all the pies' knot. Where a conformist pupil will wrap the tie around the central knot once, the wag will wrap it around three, four, even five times, so that the thing around their necks resembles less a tie, more a fat, motionless toad. This technique has been around since the 1970s (at least), and is the preferred option of the brutish.

More insidiously and cleverly rebellious is the 'long thin-bit' technique. The conventional tie-wearer will allow the fatter end of the tie predominance, so the spindlier end lodges silent and unnoticed behind its more pompous sibling. The clever naughty boy or girl will turn this convention on its head, leaving the fat end a stubby irrelevance, while the thin part indulges itself in a display of barefaced length.

More brilliant still is the relatively recent technique of 'tie colour customisation'. Where the school tie has (say) three striped colours, and one of these colours offends the wearer, they will pluck it out, fibre by painstaking fibre, so just the colours of which the wearer approves remain.

The fact that students are using such ingenuity to subvert the wearing of ties suggests that they recognise them for what they are: a pointlessly punitive piece of primitivism. And there are nascent signs the school tie may have had its day. They are being recognised as presenting a health and safety issue. Many is the child who, when confronted by the school bully, has been gifted ample opportunity to regret being forced to wear an adjustable noose; and in school changing rooms across the country there are red welts on teenage thighs where classmates have felt the urge to whip each other with tie ends irresistible.

Furthermore, the necktie is a germ's idea of utopia. I've noticed recently the fear of swine flu affecting many a student, whose response has been to hold their school tie up to their mouth and nose, oblivious to the fact that the object hasn't seen the inside of a washing machine for five whole years. So germ-ridden are these articles that doctors in hospital are no longer allowed to wear them when seeing patients.

Recognising their potential as weapons both physical and chemical, some schools have now dispensed with the tie-on tie, replacing it with the clip-on version. And it is at this empirical point in history that we take the final step from the mildly absurd into the anthropologically ridiculous. Forcing children to clip useless pieces of cloth to their neck for no discernible reason is more suited to a sketch rejected by *Monty Python* as being too surreal than it is to an education system that seeks to enlighten its pupils in the white light of rationalism.

The Iranians view the necktie as the ultimately decadent symbol of western idiocy. They are right. My sons go to a school where they are asked to wear polo shirts and a school top. They look smart, and the clothes are affordable for all. Besides, if I want my children to have the supply of blood cut off from their brain, I'll strangle them myself.

Chewing Gum

Things you don't know about chewing gum. In 1992, it was banned in Singapore. The ban proved insupportable as the criminal fraternity recognised the potential profits in gum-running, and flooded the black market with contraband merchandise from across the border with Malaysia.

As teachers, we find ourselves waging (juicy) fruitless wars against the minty stick as it lays apocalyptic waste to the undersides of desks, expensive school carpets, cupboards and curtains.

Like a cockroach sunning itself in the middle of a nuclear blast, chewing gum, once masticated, is near indestructible. Gum does not degrade after time and can cost a fortune to remove. No doubt Kim and Aggie (from *How Clean Is Your House?*) know a way to bring dirty desks back to a show-room shine with a little English mustard and elbow grease, but in the real world gum removal is the province of hydro-power, chemicals and sandblasting. Trafalgar Square was shorn of its gum deposits in 2003 at a cost of £8,500 of taxpayers' money.

My rabid aversion to gum-chewing in class may be the result of social conditioning: Papa Beadle, back in the 1970s, banned his offspring from gum of either the bubble or chewing variety. He felt it to be a display of mindless rebelliousness and, after due and deep consideration, found himself unable to allow it. My siblings and I would gaze enviously at children proudly bearing comic-clad Bazooka Joes, knowing they were never to pass our lips.

If parents make such a rule for their children nowadays (and it is one I shall be enforcing sternly with my own kids), then it is being resolutely ignored. Every desk in every school I have ever been to is, when upturned, a wasteland of glob-ules – multi-coloured, non-biodegradable muck nestling shoulder-to-shoulder, like guilty germs.

How, then, should schools fight the righteous war against the inveterate gum-chewer? Many educational institutions have a policy that bans the stuff from the whole site. But it is not a policy taken seriously by either children or teachers.

I have found myself, often, a lone voice in the howling wil-derness, recommending Stalinist purges in which every bag is searched prior to entry to the school, and all those carrying gum are immediately escorted to the Siberian salt mines, or senior detention, whichever is the least cruel.

Given that school policy on this matter is ignored, it falls to the individual classroom teacher to master the technicalities of defeating the gum-chewer. On greeting students at the door, carry with you a pleasant manner, a cheery smile and a wastepaper bin. That way, cud-munchers may deposit their sticky tasteless wads straight away, immediately aware they are entering a Zero Tolerance to Gum Zone.

The experienced teacher develops a sixth sense for chewing. Turn your back to the class to write on the board, and you can bet your bottom that you will hear the cicada-like 'drip, drip, drip' of the offending object being rolled round the mouth. Spin round with a flourish, locate the criminal and in stentorian tones direct him to the wastepaper bin.

At this point, the seasoned scallywag will secrete the oyster in a cheek pouch and deny it ever existed. He may even open his mouth unnecessarily wide, rolling his tongue around in his head to illustrate the fact that you, the teacher, are mis-taken, and there is not, nor ever was, any gum (you senile old fool). Trust yourself here. If you heard it, you heard it. If you saw, for an instant, a white wad rolling around the mouth, it is still there. No child will give up his gum without the ritual struggle, and you must be firm throughout the ceremonials.

Do not pay the slightest attention to the 'I've swallowed it' plea, for this is a shameless and barefaced lie. Any child who thinks he may, somehow, dispose of the gum without the long walk to the bin is a dreamer. Once at the bin, it takes a real technician to ensure completion. You must meet the child at the bin. Do not leave him to his own pernicious devices, for he will deceive you.

He will attempt secretively to bite off a third of his contraband, deposit it in the bin, and return to his desk with the remaining two thirds safely stowed. Greet this crime by uttering the stern (but kind) phrase 'all of it'. Repeat these words until, eventually, sometimes by tortoise-like increments, the whole stick is in the bin, and you think you have won ...

But, dear friend, you have not won! It is at just such a stage that complacency can set in, and a teacher can most easily be duped. The experienced gum-chewer will, on returning to his desk, skilfully extract another piece from his pocket and, with his back to the teacher and his smug and grinning face to the rest of the class, brazenly insert another stick. Teacher nil: student two. Keep your eyes fixed on the swift hand-to-pocket move.

Be bloody, bold and resolute, my friend. Though for each stick in the bin, a thousand will be deposited somewhere nasty, though some of us might fail and many will fall, it is a holy war we wage, and it is only through continued vigilance that the wrongdoers will be defeated, and one day we may dream of a world in which the underside of the desks are as scented, virginal and pure as the tops. In mint condition according to our definition, not theirs.

And besides, we're not allowed to smoke fags in class. Why should they be allowed to chew gum?

Boys

I didn't read Nick Hornby's *Fever Pitch* immediately it came out. I'm dimly aware, however, that it struck a chord with women. My closest female friend told me she'd found it to be a unique insight into the male psyche, before revealing, 'I'd hate to be man. It must be awful.'

Fever Pitch portrays males as hopeless creatures, all of whom are somewhere on the autistic spectrum. At the risk of reinforcing unhelpful gender stereotypes (and all women are merely a complex network of obsessions with flowers, make-up and shopping), I find it helpful, as a teacher, to remember it's the rarest of birds that sorts its record collection into chronological within alphabetical.

We boys can be prone to monomaniacal obsession; to over-enjoying the repetition of surreal and meaningless nonsense. (On a four-hour car journey last weekend, my 8-year-old son and I ripped huge fissures into my wife's psyche through fevered and non-stop repetition of the word 'bungalow'.)

There's a fun test to prove this, which can be wheeled out on INSET days: get male and female members of staff in pairs and provide them with separate envelopes containing ten human emotions. They take it in turns to mime the emotion using only facial expressions and one partner has to guess the emotion the other is portraying.

Men stink at this game. Their ability to judge another's emotional state is very poor compared to the female's skill at the same. (This inability is, I believe, a key facet of Asperger's syndrome.)

We are also rubbish at sitting still and doing what we're told: which, since this is a prerequisite of surviving the

British (or probably any) education system, can be pretty unhelpful. Boys will often drum complex rhythmic patterns on their desks, once again displaying their lack of empathy as this near-unconscious action completely disrupts everyone's learning. (On *The Unteachables*, on Channel 4, I attempted to circumvent this behaviour by providing the students with 'stress' or 'kush' balls. They squeezed the balls briefly and then hurled them in the direction of their unsurprised teacher.)

The academic effect of boys' natural antipathy towards some of the ways in which they're required to learn is that they do less well at school than girls, particularly in English. The education system has its head in its hands about this (half of it tapping its fingers in syncopated patterns).

In 2003 and 2004, I worked on a pilot project with two all-boys classes. The boys had been deemed 'at risk of underachievement'. During these two years, I learned a couple things about what makes boys tick, and how best to engage them.

The first learning point for teachers was that all-boy groups in mixed schools can work, but they are not a cure-all and have to be staffed with care. I had a quite brilliant learning support assistant, Micky, a former cabbie who spoke the same language as the kids, not just in terms of his idiom, but in that he'd been where some of the boys were, and had insight into their developing moral landscape. Much of what the boys achieved was through his role modelling of working class male values.

Secondly, you can teach empathy. Secondary teachers can be negative about the concept of 'circle time'. They assume that employing it patronises their students. What I discovered in using it over two years was that boys like to talk about their emotions, but need a safe environment to be able to do so. We did a lot of work initially on the notion of masculinity, and our differing ideas of it. In a classroom where boys feel able to express their inner insecurities safely, they will. Their profound maturity and openness would at points reduce Micky and me to near tears.

Another side effect of circle time was that it introduced, accidentally, the concept of the desk-free classroom. There's been a lot of work about this in the United States, chiefly by a guy called Michael Gurian; but it's an idea we came to pretty well independently.

I had a large classroom, so we were able to clear a central space, with the desks pushed to the sides. That way, when there was writing to be done we could disperse to the sides of the room and focus, but the majority of the classroom was given over to the central space in which all measure of kinaesthetic games could be played.

Lessons had, where possible, a kinaesthetic bias. For instance, in teaching *Macbeth* we constructed our own cauldrons or became baying Norwegian hordes. Interestingly, this actually helped with the behaviour issues. As students were not being asked to do something they were incapable of (sitting down and listening quietly), they no longer found their instincts to be in conflict with the ruling ideology of the room.

Of course, this approach relies on a good-sized classroom, but it proved to me that the thing to do with educational research and theory is to try it on. Sometimes it fits.

You can't reverse evolution in a 45-minute lesson. If boys do display characteristics associated with the spectrum of autism, there is one element of their propensity for obsession we should encourage. Autistic people have been recorded to have near superhuman powers in specific areas: the story of the 'idiot savant' who cannot relate well to other humans, but who is able to draw a technically accurate picture of Chartres Cathedral from memory is well known. There is an argument that within each boy there is a bit of the idiot savant. As an English teacher you are aware of nouns (idiot) being stolid, unchangeable labels and adjectives (savant) as fluid, therefore more optimistic.

With boys, our focus should be on celebrating and developing the adjective, rather than punishing the noun.

Fear and Loathing

Thwock! The class shudders. The punitive teacher has entered the room and you can bet your life he has zero tolerance of low-level bad behaviour. He casts a Lee Van Cleef sneer at each corner of the room, before delivering the line, in resonant basso profundo: 'Fear me!'

Meanwhile, in a classroom somewhere down the corridor, children are laughing. Little Miss Child-centred is being lovely and loved accordingly.

There are two main methods of managing the behaviour in a classroom: 'Fear me!' and 'Love me.' Both require a bit of brass neck. (Only one requires an exclamation mark.) Children may feel inclined to refuse either instruction. 'No, I won't fear you,' says John, 'for you are not at all scary.' Or 'I find myself unable to give you the love you so desperately seek, teacher. You're not worthy of affections as discerning as mine. (Moreover, I didn't think you were meant to enter this profession to make up for the lack of emotional nourishment you have in your own paltry, unhappy little life.)'

Newish teachers will be familiar with the 'don't smile until Christmas' recommendations handed down by seasoned members of staff, the 'get-your-retaliation-in-first', Roy Keane approach to discipline.

Roy, in his early years as a professional midfield enforcer, used to employ the technique of 'cementing'. On the 'w' of the whistle, when faced with a new midfield opponent, he would, with little ceremony or introduction, 'cement him'. This left his now sorely bruised opposite number in little doubt that Roy was indeed the doughtiest of opponents.

So it is in the classroom of the enforcer. Step out of line and you're gonna get cemented. Every infraction, however minor, is firmly stamped on.

This 'they don't like it up 'em' approach to managing a class may well work. (I've never managed it myself. I tried not smiling until Christmas, but lasted ten minutes into period one, when a year eight boy told a gag about David Beckham going into a library.)

You've got to have the certainty of your convictions to maintain a stone face for three-and-a-half months, and you've also got to be pretty certain you are infallible. There's no place for apologies in a punitive teacher's classroom.

Besides this, chasing up detentions is horrifically hard work. The punitive teacher who does it all by the book doesn't get home until very late indeed. His home time is spent writing reports that say things like: 'And at this point Jason tutted.' By which time the practitioner of the 'love me' method has fed the cat, watched a bit of telly and read a book to her own children.

She has achieved all this by using one technique above all others – praise, and lots of it. Praise is the surest, most positive, utterly foolproof way of keeping a classroom full of young people focused on the reason they are in a classroom.

There is room for delicate censure, even a place for gentle upbraiding, but I find accentuating the positive does indeed, to quote Uncle Bing, eliminate the negative, and moreover leaves very little room for messing with the in-between.

Everyone likes praise. Even at 40, it only takes Mrs Beadle to mention for the third time that evening that I make a lovely cup of tea to ensure that I run, once again the gleeful dupe, in the direction of the kettle.

Praise envy exists, and can be exploited. Settling a class that has just returned from a combined cock-fighting and bear-baiting session at lunch is best done by exploiting such petty jealousies. Should you have your tables grouped, lavishing effusive praise on the first table to be settled ensures the rest follow suit. 'Cripes,' thinks the naughty table (which is of one mind), 'that lot are getting praise. I want some of that. I'd better sit down and divest myself of my outdoor wear in double-quick time.' The focus of praise, however, should be on work rather than behaviour, since work is what we are there to do, and behaving as a civilised human being is a prerequisite to getting such work done. The praise of such endeavour can take place publicly or in private. They are of equal value.

Student teachers would benefit greatly from watching the film *Bill & Ted's Excellent Adventure*. In what is unarguably the second greatest philosophical treatise ever committed to celluloid (marginally less brilliant than the utterly profound and totally unrelated *Bill and Ted's Bogus Journey*), two slacker Californian teenagers found a new and infinitely better society based on the lyrics of their fictional heavy metal band, Wyld Stallyns. The motto of this society, in which peace and love rule and war is a forgotten nonsense, is: 'Be excellent to each other ... dude.'

Imagine, if you will, the teaching course that includes a 'being excellent to one another' component. This could take the form of weekly, timetabled praise practice. Student teachers would sit in a circle and take it in turns to say lovely things to each other. These sessions could be themed. We could laud each other's appearance one week, say positive things about comportment the next. By the time graduates of such a course enter the classroom they would be fluent in the language of praise, and consequently in class management.

If we smile at people, they smile back. If someone makes you feel good, you will be good. And if you've got a bag full of carrots, you'll find you don't actually need the stick.

As a professional, and a near-sentient member of the human race, I have had enough of politicians promulgating the repulsive dogma of zero tolerance. Enforcing discipline is not of the same value as allowing young people to locate it in themselves. And tolerance is infinitely more likely to work than its antithesis.

Waterloo Road

The pneumatic head teacher used to be a prostitute. Photos from that period of her life have fallen into the wrong hands and she is being blackmailed by one of the architects tendering for the new school building. One of the English teachers who, last term, took up with a single mum, now finds her to have disappeared off the face of the earth, leaving him to bring up her two teenage daughters on his own.

And the French teacher? Having only recently surfaced from an unsatisfying dalliance with lesbianism, she has legally adopted a former pupil, who is a heroin addict.

Waterloo Road sounds far-fetched until you put it up against real life. I once had a brief exchange with an immaculately clad and apparently sublimely professional member of middle management, who asked me whether the fact that he was whacked out on ketamine at 8.45 a.m. showed? And I had substantial professional respect for the teacher whose approach to marking mock exams was to throw the lot directly in the bin and then give them the grade he felt like giving them.

All human life can be found in British schools, and those towards the bottom of the pile, as Waterloo Road decidedly is, attract a rich brew of staff, from committed, passionate ideologues determined to change the class system one child at a time; through careerist zealots whose passion is reserved for their sports car; into characters whose tenure on sanity is weaker than a one-day-old lamb. Whilst it is unlikely that the events that happen to the staff at Waterloo Road would take place within the same six-week period, given a bit more time they inevitably occur.

But where the programme gets it right in a way that no other cinematic snapshot of schools has got anywhere near is in its representation of the pupils and of their relationships with the staff. I recognise the kids in Waterloo Road: their fragile emotional lives, their brushes with authority, their favoured wind-up of the week and their problematic home lives. And, most of all, I recognise the compassionate way with which their teachers deal with them. When watching the new series, when a child is in genuine trouble and it is a teacher that they turn to, note that the teacher speaks to the child with empathy, concern and a genuine desire to do the right thing for them. They try, and usually get it somewhere near right.

So, Waterloo Road is a version of reality, an extreme one admittedly, but they have clearly done their homework on making it feel like the real thing. It does. With one exception. In real schools there's far more shagging.

Literacy

Blaming the Sector Before You

My year elevens can't tell a comma from a colon. They write in three different tenses in the space of a single sentence and think that a preposition is something to do with asking someone out. Of course, it's all their last teacher's fault. I blame him.

The trouble is, Mark's a good teacher: he's personable, intelligent, passionate and devoted to the kids, so it can't really be his fault, can it? We'll have to look further afield. Mark informs me that it was actually all the fault of the teacher before him; that they didn't get much of a crack of the whip in year nine. So, we have our scapegoat and, having shifted the blame away from ourselves, can get on with another nourishing bout of box-ticking and filling in of round-robins.

I raised the issue of the education they received in year nine with the class themselves. (If you want a decent view of something in British education, it's always best to ask the kids.) They assure me that their teacher in year nine was excellent. They had her for both years eight and nine; and she really pushed them. They remain genuinely and humblingly grateful to her, stating, en masse and emphatically, that she was the sole reason they achieved such great SATs results.

Their year seven teacher is still at the school. She tells me that they came to her with ridiculously inflated SATs results from key stage two. She even recalls looking at the data sheet for them over four years ago and mouthing, 'Strewth. That child's never a level five all the time I've got a hole in my bum.' She's got a theory, and it's a seductive one for any secondary schoolteacher in search of a scapegoat. 'Primary schoolteachers are all idiots,' she mutters to me, careful that no one else is listening in. 'They can't write themselves, so don't have the ability to teach children how to do it.'

It's seductive, sure enough, but it's nonsense. I was lucky enough to meet Ros Wilson a couple of years ago. She clarified things for me: over the summer holidays kids can lose, albeit temporarily, as much as two NC levels; they haven't done any work on literacy for six weeks, and so are understandably a bit rusty after they transfer to secondary. Secondary teachers' claim that the grades are inflated isn't true. The kids quickly regain the knowledge they'd acquired at primary school within a couple of weeks of getting back in the swing of things.

Besides, having sat in on one of Ros's training sessions on the 'Big Writing', I'm pretty certain that writing is taught in primary schools in a much more structured and successful way than it is in secondaries. So, I can't blame the kids' teachers in year six, nor years five down to one.

And it certainly won't be the nurseries any more, given that the strictures of the Statutory Framework for the Early Years Foundation Stage Goals suggests nursery school kids should be writing well-punctuated sentences.

And so, who is left to blame? Blaming parents is too much the raddled old cliché. Educational establishments blaming parents, who, after all, only want the best for their children, for a lack of educational attainment is counterproductive. It changes nothing and allows people who should be working together for the same goals to sit on sidelines, tutting.

Blaming the midwives seems a little unfair, and so, through a near platonic process of rationale and reasoning, I have come to a resolute conclusion as to where responsibility lies for my year eleven class's inability to construct a decent sentence: I blame their uncles! If those feckless swines had shown a little more interest in their nieces and nephews at an earlier age, we wouldn't be in the state we are in now. And I propose a whole raft of initiatives with snappy titles focused on getting uncles into schools.

Blaming the previous teacher is something we have all done at some point, but I've noticed though that this seemingly venal little sin is not just one committed by individuals, it is the temptation to which whole sectors cannot say no.

Witness the briefing I was given for a speech I gave for a further education organisation last week. The third point I was asked to cover was, 'What responsibility should schools have in preparing students for Further Education? Why are pupils leaving schools not fully literate or numerate?' And the temptation to answer this with, 'Well, of course, it's entirely the fault of the teacher before me … and the sector before yours,' was irresistible.

An interesting solution to this 'knee-jerk-that-gets-us-nowhere' comes from an unexpected place. I had given a speech to a group of army basic skills tutors the week before (and, yes, one of them did tell me, 'Get your 'aircut. You 'orrible little man'). Following on from my own 45-minute diatribe, a moustachioed brigadier stood casually in front of a lectern and spoke more sense on this subject in two minutes than I have heard from anyone in the previous 12 years. Brigadier David Wilson, Director of the Army Educational and Training Branch, inspired his tutors by asking them to take responsibility for failure. Army basic skills tutors, stated the Brigadier, are part of a system: a system that has not equipped some of the people they work with, with proper basic skills. In taking personal responsibility for this systemic failure, the tutors also take individual responsibility for solving it. The Brigadier then went on to describe the people who work in primary and secondary schools as being, 'Brethren. We win nothing by disrespecting them.'

I felt chastened by this. Chastened by my own prejudice (the British army is perhaps not the first place I would go to seek enlightenment), and further chastened by the fact that the Brigadier's liberalism casts my own blame-shifting into fresh relief as the horror it is.

Who, then, is responsible for the failure of my class to master the comma? According to the Brigadier, I am. And you know what? He's right. I'd better get my finger out.

It's Political Correctness Gone Mad!

Society has changed greatly since the eighties. Shoulder pads are now viewed as a sign of inadequacy and woe betide the man who rolls the sleeves of his jacket up to the elbows. If you were to write in defence of being free with the many contrived moralities of language in those days, you would first have to nail your PC colours to the mast. 'Some of my best friends are black/gay/disabled (delete as appropriate), but ...'

Today, it's the obverse. This article is written in defence of teaching children the existence of political correctness. Not teaching them that it is right or wrong. It's not a teacher's job to draw the conclusions. But that it exists. However, in order to speak of political correctness nowadays, in anything other than a negative light, you first have to brandish your anti-PC qualifications, so you don't appear a blind and foolish proponent of its pogroms.

As anyone who has stared unflinchingly into the vacant eyes of 'PC gone mad' will tell you, it's as terrifying, and as totalitarian, as its supposed antithesis. Servicing the needs of social workers in a now infamous social services department of a north London council was a bleak period for me. Once, on a training day, I made the mortal error of being bashful when someone had complimented my handwriting. Blushing, unused to being the recipient of anything like praise in that environment, I said, 'Oh, thanks. I think I've got the handwriting of a 17-year-old girl.' My colleague found just enough time to turn purple, before rushing gleefully to submit a written complaint about the many unacceptable 'isms' in my innocent expression.

I also attended a training day at which a Caucasian lady prefaced every statement with, 'As a black woman I think ...' 'But you're white,' I screamed inwardly, 'You're white. Why does nobody have the bravery to point this out? And if you can't even recognise your own ethnicity, who cares what you think?'

In practice, political correctness became the thing it set out to combat. The exact point on the circle at which far right and far left meet and merge, there is no dogma in a PC environment but the holy dogma that there is no dogma.

Its heart though may well have been in the right place at a point before it became jealousy with a halo. It sought to protect people, mainly minorities, from the impact of words, be they thoughtless or mindful. Sadly, in doing so, it punished others. Most dialect versions of English, and often Standard English itself, are intrinsically racist. We have a thousand unpleasant slang terms for black people, with just the innocuous 'honky' kicking its legs blithely in the air at the other end of the see-saw. The phrase 'honest injun', for instance, has been part of my own argot since childhood. I never thought to question its morality. It was just something that people from London said to emphasise that they were telling the truth. But in the realms of the politically correct such dialect forms are outlawed. This leaves us in the paradoxical position of upholding as sacrosanct immigrant children's right to use their own language, at the same time as banning indigenous children from using theirs.

Why then, would anyone be prepared to take a stand against prevailing thought and speak up for teaching political correctness in the classroom? As a small child I remember being in receipt of another form of idiocy, the brain-dead, sing-song naivety of 'sticks and stones may break my bones, but names will never hurt me'. Given the choice between a whack round the leg with a twig, or a mean-spirited comment about my appearance or family, I'd argue that the callous word causes more lasting damage. Words can hurt like hell.

My north London council colleagues would refer, without sniggering, to a thing called 'the language of equality'. And if you ignore its somewhat clumsy title, I think there's still a place for the ideas behind this outmoded expression. It's useful for kids – day-to-day practitioners of language – to know such a system exists.

Take, for instance, the phrase 'AIDS victim'. During the early 1990s there was a drive to tag people who had acquired the human immunodeficiency virus as 'living with HIV', as opposed to being 'victims' of it. There are few, outside the most militant political group, who would argue with this drive. The word victim implies defencelessness and defeat, whereas 'living with' suggests that the fat lady hasn't even begun tuning up yet, and that the person in question is vital, active, getting on with the task of living, and not the passive recipient of an immediate death sentence.

At the risk of drawing the rabid wrath of the anti-PC brigade, I think children should be given the opportunity to experiment with these ideas; to think about whether being considerate in their expression is a good thing. And it is possible to teach the existence of a more considerate version of expression in a disinterested manner, raising it as a possibility to consider at the same time as satirising its extremities. Kids love being asked to define their own politically correct expressions, and respond with glee to describing a baldy as being folically challenged, and a porker as being calorifically enhanced.

Study of this subject causes them to investigate the intrinsic morality of their own language, and to see how this may have changed over the years. It also politicises. A black girl who comes to the realisation that Standard English is the language of a white male orthodoxy, which unconsciously monopolises accepted forms of expression in order to perpetuate their right to rule, is a young lady who may well be motivated to do something about this in her own life.

Censorship of ideas is the realm of the idiot. Banning ideas such as political correctness from the classroom is as Stalinist, doltish and clumsy as the code itself.

So, yes, I admit it. I am in favour of political correctness being taught in schools. But, then I would be. I am a *Guardian*-reading schoolteacher who has lived in Stoke Newington, has a bottle of extra virgin olive oil out on display next to the cooker and, I am utterly ashamed to say, have not only eaten couscous, but thoroughly enjoyed it.

Learning from the Enemy

I am in the middle of filming a Channel 4 series about adult literacy at the mo. It's brought up a couple of issues that seem to have a contemporary kind of chime I'd like to show and tell. That is, how each sector of British education holds the others as being the realm of the amateur.

I'll hold my head in my hands and 'fess up that I too have succumbed to the shameful stereotype that primary school-teachers are all intellectual lightweights, obsessed with bunny rabbits, cuddles and fluffy clouds; that they have a little knowledge about everything, and that they wouldn't cut it in the harsher environment of the hormone-riddled behavioural nightmare of the secondary school corridor. For their part, many practitioners in the primary sector regard the secondary teacher as being a feckless, lazy waster whose specialist interest in their subject automatically precludes them from having any real interest in, or talent for, dealing with the emotional lives of children. They are right of course.

The lack of will for practitioners from either sector to engage with the specific difficulties of the other means that we fail to learn from each other, and the chief victims of this cold war are the people we teach.

On entering the realms of adult literacy this antipathy from one sector towards the other is even more pronounced. Since their only contact with the graduates of our school system is with the hordes of people whom it has failed to equip with useable basic skills, they tend to regard the humble schoolteacher as being a retrograde incompetent, who is blithely unaware of the questionable grails of learning styles (cough), hemispheric dominance (harrumph) and Brain Gym (double splutter with a phlegmy cough attached). They are right of course, and their assertions appear all too plausible until you enter an adult literacy class in which nobody learns anything at all, and even worse, there is neither any attempt to teach anything nor understanding of the fact that this might be important.

The full horror of each sector casting a snook at the others is in the vastness of the opportunities to learn from each other that we are missing. Gary Lineker[11] said something once about Terry Venables[12] that I've always found very tenable.[13] Lineker, an intelligent man, and a sublimely expert practitioner in his field, said that at the point Venables was appointed England manager, no coach had taught our Gary anything he didn't know about the technical skills of being a centre forward for several years. I know that to compare oneself with Lineker is the height of self-delusion (I tend to regard myself more as teaching's equivalent of Stan Bowles,[14] good on his day but unreliable over a whole season), but Lineker's words rang with me. With the exception of one quiet word in my shell-like from Sir William

---

[11] England's finest ever centre forward.

[12] England's finest ever manager, sacked because he didn't do auditions.

[13] See what I did there?

[14] Lazy, gambling addict centre forward from the great QPR side of the mid-1970s. My childhood hero. Was often found in the bookies five minutes before kick-off.

Atkinson,[15] I have not learnt anything of any real use from anyone in the secondary sector since my third year of teaching.

In the space of seven weeks working with experts from primary and adult sectors, however, I've acquired more new knowledge and skills than in the previous five years combined. Sue Lloyd and Sara Wernham's 'Jolly Phonics' system is a work of unparalleled magic with which you can teach children to read in 15 seconds flat, 'Toe by Toe' has had a huge impact on my own son's reading and a well thumbed copy of Cynthia Klein's *Unscrambling Spelling* should be in the back pocket of every secondary school English teacher in the country. Tomorrow I meet with Ros Wilson, firebrand originator of 'Punctuation Kung Fu' and 'Big Writing'. I can barely contain my excitement, my lifelong love of learning reignited.

If I had remained cloistered in my secondary school classroom, spitting jealously at the infinitesimal marking burden of the primary schoolteacher, all the time thanking the heavens I knew what a free period was, I would have remained ignorant of these genius practitioners. As a secondary English teacher I have always been concerned that those pupils who enter my class unable to read and don't leave it in the same state. A ten-minute chat with a primary schoolteacher may have resulted in another conclusion.

And the point here is that, for once, the DfES Innovation Unit is piloting a radical initiative which, if followed through to its conclusion, is liable to revolutionise education in this country: the all-through school. A system with real vision

---

[15] Knighted head teacher of the Phoenix School, which is the nearest school to QPR's ground. More substantial than Stan Bowles. Rarely, if ever, found in the bookies.

would see the all-through school as the inevitable future, not just so the kids don't have to go through petrifying transitions, but so that each sector can learn from the other's brilliance, so that schools are cohesive environments in which all approaches to teaching and learning are known and in which the phrase 'joined-up thinking' is something more than the ultimate in risible governmental and management cliché.

Adult Literacy

The government has poured an unprecedented amount of money into adult literacy. It is an unglamorous area, described by a television producer as 'The Cinderella Sector', and one unlikely to win over too many voters in the shires. They have hit all the targets early, and you can bet the Tories wouldn't be making this a priority area. So, why then, in the Channel 4 series *Can't Read, Can't Write*, which finished last night, was I not just standing back and applauding the work of the many dedicated, skilled and underpaid adult literacy teachers? Was the seemingly scripted dribble of invective consistently forming on my lower lip merely the 'poorly informed' utterances of a committed self-publicist?

Perhaps.

Or you could choose to see another side of the truth. During the filming of the series I wrote an article about what I had learned from a dyslexia expert, Cynthia Klein, whose spelling strategies, though sadly not the lady herself, featured in the programme. I had encountered a pale and watered-down version of these in school, but in getting them from the source, they were obviously significantly useful in secondary schools. In working with Cynthia and other adult literacy experts, it was obvious that a secondary school English teacher could learn much from them. Questions formed: why doesn't every PGCE course feature just one day where prospective teachers learn strategies to deal with students with dyslexia? Why do kids have an 'entitlement' to a balanced curriculum when they can't read? What is the point of teaching geography, for instance, to an illiterate pupil when you could be teaching them to read? The article concluded that there is much that the school sector could learn from some adult literacy professionals.

A year on, I voice the forlorn hope that this could be a two-way process, and that the policy makers and curriculum designers from the National Institute of Adult Continuing Education (NIACE) and the National Research and Development Centre for Adult Literacy and Numeracy could pick up something from people in the schools sector, particularly from the nation's experts in how to teach people to read, most of whom are to be found at the Reading Reform Foundation.

Sadly, it does not appear this is possible. With what I have found to be a characteristic closed mindedness, NIACE's response to the issues raised in the programme have been to release a statement, featuring a shocker of a spelling error, and using the comments of a television reviewer as back-up. The gist of which is, 'Don't trust a word this man says. He is not an academic, he's got messy hair, and they are only opinions.'

Since they would obviously benefit from a lesson in this, I shall separate the facts from opinions for them.

Fact: there are no teaching materials for people who cannot read or write at all. Opinion: perhaps there should be.

Fact: the teaching materials do not have a structured and complete course of synthetic phonics at any level. Opinion: maybe they should have.

Fact: people with learning difficulties and learning disabilities are placed in the same class. Opinion: this is not likely to help those with learning difficulties to view themselves as being anything other than stigmatised by the people they are approaching to relieve them of the stigma.

Fact: the teaching materials are based on a balance of speaking and listening, reading and writing. Opinion: teaching people who can already speak English perfectly well how to speak English is a bit of a waste of time.

Fact: they are handing out certificates in literacy, which are 'broadly equivalent' to a GCSE pass where there is no assessment of writing. Opinion: oh, so that's how they've hit their targets!

It can be difficult for academics to take the humble conclusions of the classroom practitioner seriously, particularly one who is parading his adult literacy version of an NQT year in front of a reality TV show. 'Research!' they are minded to cry. 'Research above all things.' However, aside from the probably inadmissible argument that the six months I spent with my students could be described as ethnographic, research itself can be slanted. Apparently, 90 percent of people on adult literacy courses are happy with the course. To which I'd reply that if you'd spent a lifetime tainted by academic failure and were given a badge for something you could already do, and were then asked whether you were happy, you'd probably be ticking the top box.

I go back to the idea of sectors learning from each other. I learned a lot from Cynthia Klein; I hope that some of the policy makers are not so assured of their moral superiority in all things educational to miss the opportunity of learning from their colleagues in the primary school sector. The mechanics of learning to read are the same if you are 6 or 60. It does not infantilise adults by teaching them to read using kids' methods; it infantilises them playing the silly guessing games they call whole word recognition without any previous grounding in phonics. Foolish indeed is the individual, organisation or sector that begins to think they have special skills no one else could understand.

Boys' Reading

It isn't that well known that the much publicised gender gap in attainment is concentrated in and caused by boys' underperformance in one subject: English. The male half of the school population competes perfectly well with their fairer classmates in both science and maths. The problems are in the literacy-based subjects and are partially caused by the fact that given the choice of a rumble or a read, boys will choose the former.

Gary Wilson, in what is without doubt the seminal text on this subject, *Breaking through Barriers to Boys' Achievement*, argues convincingly for the setting up of special 'Boyzones' in libraries, in which books are presented as dangerous, taboo and most definitely not for the girls. He tells the tale of one school library which even went so far as to encase certain books in faked barbed wire on the ceiling, along with a sign telling boys that they were not allowed, under any circumstances, to take them out! Needless to say when the wire came down, the books flew into the schoolbags of boys eager to consume them.

This week every maintained school in England will be asked to choose 20 free books from a list of 170 titles created by the School Library Association, so that they may start the construction of their own 'Boyzone'. Whoever created this list, and I detect Wilson's hand, has done their homework. The books are grouped together under imaginative, boy-friendly titles: there are books to make you explore, discover, fear and even to boogle!

Given a chance to scrutinise someone else's list of what constitutes a good read, it's inevitable anyone will play the 'why isn't my favourite in there?' game. There will be the odd question as to whether Jeremy Clarkson is a proper role model for boys. To which the answer would be of course he is: proper geezer, likes motors, writes up a storm. There will be those who would question the presence of Ricky Gervais's money-making exercise *Flanimals of the Deep*, alongside several versions of what Wilson himself satirises as the whoppinggreatbookoffactsflickers. But the production of this list at least engages with the fact that boys need to see reading as a pleasurable experience within which there is a special space for them, no girls allowed. It's a start, and a bloody good one at that. Put your Leavisite snobbishness aside and dive in.

Literature

Education for Leisure[16]

Carol Ann Duffy once touched my knee. Not out of suggestion (heavens no), more in concern, in empathy; a chimp's consolation of another in pain. It was during a session for teachers she was running in which we shared our piffling scrabbles at verse, and my own attempt revealed an emotional scar, too livid, too recent to be properly the subject of easy discussion.

I resolved never to wash the knee again, and have lived that promise. It makes bathing difficult and I've had to entirely give up on the idea of ever showering again, but it has its consolations: like Quentin Crisp before me I have found that after a year the dirt doesn't really accumulate, and my perma-caked and by-now-slightly-rotting knee stands for me as a daily testament to the utter regard in which I, and many other teachers of English Literature, hold both the lady and her work.

Duffy's poem 'Education for Leisure', which has lived a relatively blameless life on the AQA literature syllabus for several years now, is as complicated or as simple as you wish to make it. In it, the narrator, who is more likely young than old, is obsessively concerned with recognition, but has no real understanding that such recognition is more likely to be achieved through some worked and nurtured creative ability than its obverse. It (the narrator) craves fame, and

---

[16] This was never published. The issue with topical stuff is its topicality can run out before you've finished the article.

launches into a procession of ever escalating violence(s) in the search for such notoriety.

It is a very funny poem. But in amongst the cracking gags, 'I pour the goldfish down the bog. I flush the chain. I see that it is good,' my faulty eye for these things tells me that this poem is satirical of the *Pop Idol* generation and of our unquestioning worship of fame; it is about the result of ego being denied substance for its existence; about creativity and its relationship with its antithesis; about what it is to occupy the underclass; and, crucially, it is concerned with the psychology of young people who might be of the mind-set to experiment with the idea of taking a carving knife for a run outside the house and seeing what sparks fly.

One of the many substantial joys of teaching poetry is that it is in no way binary. There is always the beauty of doubt in any interpretation, but while rejoicing in this, I would hesitate to make an apologetically definitive statement about Duffy's work, and that is: it most certainly isn't a call to arms for suggestible idiots. That is rarely how poetry works.

I, and my colleagues in English departments across the country, use Duffy's work in the way that (we hope) it is meant to be used. As a prompt for discussion of what it is that conspires to create the accidental murderer, as perhaps the only chance we are allowed to discuss such a psychology. Duffy's poem gives teachers an opportunity to discuss with our students their fears about knife crime; fears of being recipient or deliverer of the blade. And in discussing such fears, we find we are able to rationalise them and, maybe, just maybe, not act out on them.

For the AQA to have caved in to a single philistine complaint about the poem shows an uncharacteristic lack of bravery, logic and vision. The anthology in which 'Education for

Leisure' has sat for many years is, for me, the most beautifully constructed resource in British education; and aside from those who teach it, the most valuable. It sits in the schoolbags of most 15- and 16-year-olds, and I will not be alone as an English teacher in voicing a long overdue thanks for the impact this poetry has had on my students, and for the profound questions it has caused them to ask of themselves.

Duffy's dignified answer draws attention, in the form of the poem 'Mrs Schofield's GCSE', to the bloodlust that even the most cursory look at a collected works of Shakespeare would reveal, and surely the exceptional people at the AQA would not be blind to the irony implicit in the question asked by AllyF, a particularly astute contributor to Comment is Free, as to whether we still teach Browning's 'My Last Duchess' or 'The Laboratory', which feature murderous intent, jealousy and honour killing. The answer, Ally, is that both these poems nestle just a few pages away from 'Education for Leisure' in the same anthology.

Within Duffy's response though there is a line pulsing with righteous anger, 'Something is rotten in the state of Denmark – do you know what this means?' An accusation of idiocy fully substantiated by the response of Pat Schofield, an exams invigilator (who may or may not be a qualified teacher), and who made the initial complaint: 'I think it is absolutely horrendous,' says Pat, 'What sort of message is that to give to kids who are reading it as part of their GCSE syllabus?'

Well Pat, since you ask, it is the message that we think highly of the children we teach, that they are able to distinguish between the voice of the narrator and the meaning of the work. Do you know what this means? We are certain the children we teach will come up with a mature and thoughtful response to the issues the poem allows us to investigate. A message far removed from the message they'll get from adults teaching that them it is OK to ban or burn books and poems.

Andrew Motion

Flipping 'eck. Give a man a pitiful stipend and 150 bottles of sherry a year and he starts thinking he has to earn it.

Andrew Motion's public pronouncements on the study of British poetry, once again, give new meaning to the phrase, 'Leave it out Grandad. You've never taught in a blooming school, let alone followed the AQA syllabus.'

So when Motion argues that poets Simon Armitage and Carol Ann Duffy are a little tired and should be carted off to the remaindered list, perhaps to be replaced by John Agard, there is the worry that a few too many of those 150 bottles have been taken in one sitting. John Agard is, erm, already on the curriculum.

Motion's argument is that the canon of English literature is in permanent need of updating, and that what is on the school curriculum should be changed regularly to encompass new voices. His admirable intent appears to be to broaden the curriculum so that it encompasses the full polyphony of differing poetries available; and that some of these should be voices of differing cultural heritage.

Fair enough. But praise here where praise is due, the AQA's selection of 'Poems from Different Cultures', which all students of that syllabus must study, includes work by 14 different poets from 10 different countries; one of whom is John Agard. (Incidentally, only one of these multi-cultural poets has found their way into Motion's Poetry Archive.) The place of these poems on the curriculum allows students the chance to form emotional responses to slavery and apartheid; to displacement, drought, disparity; to the complex inter-relationship between evil and love; and to the idea that religion might be groundless superstition. They examine cultural and linguistic heritage and the conscious homogenising of acceptable modes of discourse by an elite white male orthodoxy. Yeh, I know I'm going on a bit here, but the point is, I don't think Senior Examiners at the AQA drew the poets' names on the back of a beer mat during a particularly boozy lunch.

The same with Armitage and Duffy; poets whose work is both accessible and complex and, as such, sublimely relevant. I have lost count of the number of students who have cried at the climax of Armitage's 'November', or girls who have begun to form a new version of femininity in their heads as a result of reading Duffy.

His caveat, 'I know teachers are overworked, but ...' paints us as slightly doltish, too stressed out to form an opinion on the books we teach; and his supposition that teachers may be tired of teaching the same texts does both us and our students disservice. It may be the twentieth time I have read *Macbeth*, but it is always my students' first, and I relish the fact that years spent studying it have allowed me and other teachers to develop expertise.

It is good that the Poet Laureate sees himself as a voice for new poets, and yes the canon is not and should not be static, nor exclusively dead, white or male; but perhaps in promoting newness and arguing for Armitage and Duffy to join the subs bench, he might want to compare these poets to Ryan Giggs who, when told Man United were signing a new winger, retorted, 'He'd better be good.'

If he wants to take something in the English curriculum on, then perhaps the list of approved pre-1914 authors might be a better place from which to start chopping bark off a dead canon. Every student I've ever taught, when confronted with choices as enlivening as Bunyan's 'An Exhortation to Peace and Unity' or Defoe's 'Journal of a Plague Year', has found their celebratory dance all too easy to suppress.

Politics and Policy

Teaching on the Cheap

One of the disappointments of advancing years, alongside beginning to look like the least handsome of your two grandmothers and teaching with your right palm permanently pushed into the small of your back in case a disintegrating vertebra decides to pop out, is the final, sorry realisation that everything that ever happens in the world, ever, is entirely motivated by money.

The first widescreen coalition policy announcements are, as is the way of all things, entirely concerned with lucre and its redistribution away from the pockets of schoolteachers. The announcement that any primary or secondary school that has been judged as outstanding by OFSTED can be fast-tracked to academy status, and that there could be up to 2,900 new academies in operation by the beginning of the next academic year, far from being not 'thought through', as Head of the Association of Teachers and Lecturers, Mary Bousted, has it, is a supremely calculated, ideological step on a journey started in the 1970s by Lord Baker to make educating children more financially efficient.

Anyone interested in the background to this could do worse than read Nick Davies's *The School Report*. In it, Davies interviews the good Lord who, from an armchair in his 'dazzlingly beautiful' Sussex home, admits that key to his own policy changes was a desire to watch local education authorities (LEAs), 'wither on the vine' and that local management of schools was adopted because 'it diminished the power of the teacher unions and LEAs'. He stops only to add, 'They hate me. Ah-huh-huh-huh.'

The proposed grand scale conversion of successful local authority schools to academy status is motivated entirely by that same instinct. By implementing a system that requires education to be funded by the state, but controlled by an ever increasing number of voluntary sector sponsors, they destroy the unions' ability to negotiate pay and conditions centrally and, in doing so, make it virtually impossible to retain any cohesive national pay agreement. If you doubt this, observe a recent op-ed piece in *The Telegraph* by Stephen Pollard, editor of the *Jewish Chronicle*. Making reference to the 'educational establishment', which he lists as 'educationalists, teaching unions, bureaucrats and local education authorities', Mr Pollard donates a vehemently expressed piece of advice for the Secretary of State: 'Unless Mr Gove outmanoeuvres – for which, read "destroys" – that educational establishment, he will fail because it will fight him. Relentlessly.'

We are sold this under the dazzle camouflage that academies drive up standards and that those educational standards are the sole motivation of the new government's actions. Firstly, whilst a few academies, such as the one in which I worked last year, see a substantial rise in the number of students gaining five A* to C grades, this is against a background of the majority being vastly less successful. Secondly, and as no one has pointed out, the initial tranche of schools that Gove and Cameron are seeking to improve have already been judged as outstanding whilst under local authority control, and probably don't really need their standards being driven up a further minuscule amount.

It may be they do well because the staff are happy, that they are properly paid and are happy to give of themselves because the head has not thought to destroy any semblance of a home life by the insane and inhuman workloads that can be some teachers' experience of academy status.

There is a long-held view by many who comment on education that teachers' salaries are quite simply vastly too expensive; some of the ICT evangelists, in particular, suggest that the skilled and nuanced human touch of the able teacher could be easily replaced by a vastly cheaper ICT solution. And, economically at least, they have a strong argument. Historically, teaching has been a middle class profession, attracting relatively well educated, empowered and, crucially, left-wing entrants. This has made the teaching profession, and particularly its strong union representation, anathema to the right, by whom they are seen as a too expensive irritation, and ideal candidates for being broken upon the rack of the initiative.

This policy also signals a key ideological change in the academies programme. Under Labour they were meant to replace 'failing' schools, predominantly in poor areas, and indeed the one key success of the programme has been to make schools that often serve run down communities attractive to middle class parents. In achieving this, they have altered the admissions profile of these schools; and the real achievements of the programme will be seen when the new, more socially balanced intake finally graduate. Academies are, in fact, working well in terms of a social democrat remit for improving equality of opportunity for those at the bottom end of society. This policy tears up the pretence that this was in any way the key objective of academies.

One wonders whether many head teachers will display the foresight and stomach to sacrifice the additional monies on offer (for a limited period only!) for the greater good of education remaining at least partially under state control. If this policy heralds the wholesale handing over of education into private control, then, in future, schools will be run on a model of private industry where a controlling few figures will be paid ever more grotesque bonuses for keeping the workforce ever more scared and ever more poor.

Shaking the Spindlier Tree

It is possible to create an interesting 'compare and contrast' exercise using the coalition's recent education policy announcements and *The Hitchhiker's Guide to the Galaxy*. In the latter, a group of 'hyper intelligent, pan-dimensional beings' (for which read Michael Gove plus acolytes) want to know the answer to 'life, the universe and everything'. In order to do so they build the supercomputer, Deep Thought (the art of which Mr Gove thinks of most highly, and believes will be revived instantaneously by the cancelling of AS levels). Deep Thought took seven-and-a-half-million years to come up with the wrong answer; Gove is able to come up with the same quality of response far quicker.

Leaving aside the gut-wrenching disappointment that pulling the plug on Building Schools for the Future has caused communities desperate for their leaking sixties prefabs to be pulled down and replaced, little has been made of two further policy announcements that, once examined, reveal the ideological nature of what is to come in the way of cuts.

Firstly, the parallel announcement that, it appears, was designed somehow to soften the blow of many schools having to teach in leaking buildings for a further half-century:

the provision of £4 million to expand Teach First into primary schools. How this will console those communities whose schools are not now to be rebuilt is a mystery. 'Yes, we are cancelling the previous administration's plan to rebuild every school that needs it. And yes, we are dismantling state education, but that's OK, as we are going to give a few primary schools some unqualified new teachers.'

Teach First is the charity that places recent "high quality" graduates into inner city schools for a minimum of two years. Contrary to some teachers' initial reaction to the programme – 'Great! CV building for poshos' – the charity has been the cause of many bright and dedicated young people entering the profession. Teachers such as Manjit More, from Pensnett High School, who has been identified as outstanding by OFSTED and has committed himself to serving the community in the run-down part of Dudley the school serves for far more than the initial two years, and who describes himself as a 'lifer'.

The vast majority of Teach First graduates come into the profession fully cognisant of the workload entailed, and where it has been particularly successful is in importing genuine subject specialists. There are serious, expert geographers and mathematicians standing in front of inner city kids as a result of Teach First.

However, some of the claims its founder, Brett Wigdortz, is making for the programme border on the messianic; at a speech at their recent awards ceremony he appeared to claim that Teach First is the solution to feudalism in education, all the while sharing a platform with Mr Gove, the chief emissary of its reinstatement. And there is an argument that extending the programme into primary schools will be markedly less successful as those with excellent and saleable subject expertise may not want to alchemise it into the more generalist approach of the primary school all-rounder. What is more, Teach First is a charity. As such, its 'philanthropic' intent is in perfect keeping with the gibbering, see-through nonsense of Cameron's Big Society non-idea. More volunteers make for cheaper public services and Teach First graduates are not, initially at least, very well paid.

A further announcement is indicative of where the coalition have really set their sights and has sneaked out almost unnoticed: there will be no budget whatsoever next year for the training of higher level teaching assistants (HLTAs).

There is a passage in Nick Cave's most recent novel, in which he describes the modus operandi of the consummate conman. Rather than attempting to fleece those who own chattels worth stealing; rather than shaking the 'well rooted tree', the consummate conman finds it more productive to shake the spindlier tree of those who have little anyway. The poor are far easier to shake down than the middle classes.

This is a nasty, mean-spirited little cut, which can be taken as evidence of this government's desire to take away anything that supports those who have the least, and who have little voice with which to protest. Teaching assistants are generally drawn directly from the communities their schools serve. They are paid scandalously low money for a full working week, are generally there to help children with specific learning needs and have little by way of promotional prospects. In dispensing with the funding to train them to the higher level, the Training and Development Agency (TDA) condemns teaching assistants to a career of sweatshop wages with no hope of professional advancement and further denies the children they work with the chances of benefiting from their better training.

'People will still be able to gain HLTA status,' says a spokesman for the TDA, 'but the funding for training and preparation will need to be provided by the local authority from other sources. Alternatively, schools or individuals can continue to fund the training and preparation themselves.' Teaching assistants should fund their own training! From purses bulging with unspent coppers.

Here we see yet another dark side of importing the DNA of the private sector into state education. Provision for children with special educational needs can be shockingly bad in the independent sector, and they hope to bring it to the same level in state schools. It is this cut that is truly indicative of the coalition's attitude to those in society who have the most need. Quite frankly, they do not care a fig.

Welcome Mr Gove

Michael Gove is a journalist for *The Times* newspaper. He has written four books (now out of print), including a supremely toadying biography of Michael Portillo, and appears regularly on *Newsnight Review*, displaying, in heavily manicured voice, a capacity for over-loquaciousness on a seemingly limitless array of cultural matters. As a result of these endeavours he has been presented to the electorate, and to the education community in particular, as an extravagantly gifted polymath genius.

It is, perhaps, the Tories' confidence in their education spokesman's erudition and intellectual dexterity that has caused the dim birth of a collective unconscious that the Conservatives, though absent of any discernibly realistic policy in almost all other areas, have substantial strengths in their plans for education. Given then that it may be only the matter of a month before this charming man and his priestly over-assonance is in charge of the education chances of our country's young people, it is well worth a look at what bright new places Mr Gove's intellectualism will take us. Aside from constant repetition of the phrase, 'It works very well in Sweden,' what exactly are his ideas?

A recent article in the newspaper he writes for gives us valuable insight into the man, his plans and for the possible future direction of education policy in Britain. Mr Gove states, with no little pride, that the parent-led schools that will be allowed to burgeon following a Tory victory – and which Fiona Millar has revealed will be run by existing academy sponsors, or for-profit organisations, not by the parents who set them up – will be 'non-selective grammar schools'. Immediately, we wonder whether Mr Gove's much vaunted intellect was taking a day off. Since, by definition, a grammar school selects its pupils, a non-selective grammar is either a clumsy, oxymoronic non sequitur, or a weasely way of admitting that the Conservatives finally recognise that comprehensive education works. In coining this impossibly paradoxical concept, he attempts to appeal to the prejudices of his core vote, keeping selection (which even the Tories have realised is no vote winner) off the radar, whilst still appearing to be tacitly in favour of it, so as to keep the smiles from the shires still shining.

He continues with a 'standards not structures' line by taking an absurdly intrusive view of what should happen in classrooms; a proclamation of ignorance that delights in being such. 'Most parents would rather their children had a traditional education, with children sitting in rows, learning the kings and queens of England, the great works of literature, proper mental arithmetic, algebra by the age of

11, modern foreign languages. That's the best training for the mind and that's how children will be able to compete.'

Like many before him, Mr Gove conflates 'the education I had' with the education 'most parents want'. Given that his social circle is likely to include chiefly parents who purchase a version of education for their children that ensures they won't be sitting next to a child from a lower income family, it could reasonably be argued that Mr Gove has no idea whatsoever what most parents want. If he had, then he would realise it is more likely to be a 21st century education that allows children to think for themselves and equips them for the future, rather than one so firmly focused on reinstating dead tradition that it discounts any pedagogic advances made since the time of Oliver Cromwell, and regards the most important part of acquisition of knowledge, skills and understanding as being the rote learning of a series of dates.

He also proposes a committee of the 'greatest minds in Britain' – for which read anyone who has appeared on television in the role of an academic – to devise the curriculum. Carol Vorderman has already been appointed to advise maths teachers on how to teach maths! This, to use a phrase beloved of Ted Wragg, is 'beyond satire'. In summarily dismissing the talents and decisions of vastly experienced members of the education profession, most of whom have spent decades learning their trade, and ditching these in favour of the non-thoughts of the shrill lady who no longer does the sums on daytime television, Mr Gove sends out a repulsively anti-education message to both electorate and teachers alike, striking an idiot populist chime with a nation's obsession with deadhead celebrity culture.

And, just when you think the scrapings from bottom of the barrel of tradition could not be dredged any further, we get the thoughts on state education of one Charles, Prince of Wales, being held up as the exemplary voice of rich experience. The Prince, who, like most of those now pontificating on the way forward for state schools, did not attend one, and who, as the recipient of two less than excellent A levels and a lower second, would not qualify to be a teacher under the Tories' conflation of teaching ability with A level grades, is like Mr Gove, desperately concerned that the curriculum has been dumbed down! Not content with nearly prompting a constitutional crisis by using his views on 'proper' architecture to unduly influence which architect wins which tender, the Prince now believes he should have a say in what is on the curriculum, making absurd declarations as to what should be taught in schools. Mr Gove stands on the side applauding, scribbling down the Prince's ideas. 'Note to self – make deference lessons part of core curriculum.'

In Mr Gove's brave new world, the serious structural inequalities in British education will all be solved by learning poetry by rote and throwing a token Latin lesson at uncomprehending inner city kids. The near future will be characterised by a cabal of decision makers who have no experience of state education, believing they are experts, and assuming that since a 'traditional' education worked for them, a version of the same is exactly what the doctor ordered for those at the bottom of society. This is rank idiocy. On stilts. Writ large. In a shocking pink tutu. Doing the cancan. For a well-rounded and cultured intellectual, Mr Gove's pronouncements on the curriculum do a remarkably good impression of the underdeveloped views of a callow sixth former reciting prejudices at a minor public school.

Handsome Dave

We received a piece of paper through the post the other day. Beneath a picture of handsome Dave Chameleon's Roger Ramjet chin jutting heroically into a better future, there is the claim that there will be no return to selection between schools at the age of 11 under his leadership. Instead, the selection will be 'setting by ability within schools'. He goes on to say, 'Parents know it works. Teachers know it works.' This 'hold on I think I actually sniff a' policy would be brilliant, if it wasn't nonsense.

Changing his colours to suit the prevailing wind, Cameron grasps how passionate is the opposition to writing off swathes of our children as second-class citizens at an age before their abilities have bloomed. At the same time he keeps one foot in the Tory heartland. 'It's alright,' says Margo, clinking her gin against her pearls, 'that nice David Cameron has it all under control. They are keeping selection, but it's going to be within the schools.' Handsome Dave retakes the centre line, jets off to mush a team of huskies in yet another eco-friendly photo opportunity and everyone's happy.

The trouble is that he doesn't appear to have done much research on whether setting pupils by ability is actually a good thing for schools. I'll hold my hands up here. I've always been in favour of it. There are some academic benefits, and often these are most keenly felt by the lowest attaining students. Many schools limit the number of students in a group with the lowest attainment, so that they get the best pupil–teacher ratio possible. These groups will often have more in-class support and they will be able to progress at a rate suited to their needs. There's also the argument that it will bolster a school's results. A clever manager will ensure that the most experienced teachers are assigned to the class in which reside the C/D borderline students.

But this is just the appearance of progress; going up league tables because a school's whole focus is on a small cohort of students is not progress itself. It doesn't mean that the standard of educational provision school wide has improved. Mostly, the benefits of setting are to be found in the staffroom, and my own preference for it is out of pure selfishness. As Ted Wragg himself said, teaching mixed ability classes is the most difficult thing he ever did in his whole career. You have to monitor the progress of a raft of students who might include top A*s, straight Cs, C/D borderlines, plodders, early stage EAL students, the barely and preliterate. It is hellishly difficult to the point of being impossible.

It also throws up huge issues that schools which do go for setting should consider seriously. In a mixed school you will often find that setting your pupils means you have groups comprising of 25 girls and 5 boys in the top set and all-boy classes at the lower attaining end. Gary Wilson, a leading expert on boys' achievement, is also one of setting's most articulate opponents. Gary, who has overseen an exponential rise in boys' grades in Kirklees education authority, feels the impact of setting on boys' self-esteem is irreversible: 'We can tell them they're in a flexible situation and they may well believe in that, and themselves, but not for long.' There is also the issue of near-genius EAL students being automatically assigned to bottom sets in all but maths, because they can't speak English.

There is no informed consensus in our schools either for or against setting. I have taught in four different schools, all of which had subtly different attitudes to the issue, and it seems that this 'horses for courses' is the most considered.

The best way to approach the issue is to let head teachers decide what is appropriate for them and for the vision of education they have for their pupils.

Our school system is riddled with selection: by ability, by postcode and, unbelievably, also by the involuntary reflex of religious belief. If handsome Dave really wants to embrace his destiny and become the politician he could be with some genuine policies and a little less time spent in the bathroom, he should turn his attention to this.

Licensed to Teach

Lest anyone was ever in any real doubt, the recent education White Paper has made naked what the government really thinks of teachers. The time-honoured tradition of each education secretary mounting the dais to recite the statutory script, 'The current stock of teachers are the best trained, the most dedicated, the ... (yawn, where was I?)' has, with the planned introduction of licensing teachers to practice, been exposed for the sham that it is.

With recession comes the opportunity to wield a fresh broom, and the government, in the manner of the back-street spiv identifying that now might be the right time to invest for a predicted run on nylons, has observed that massed redundancies and a lack of jobs for graduates has rendered teaching seductive to 'top' graduates and unemployable bankers alike. The callow eagerness to use this opportunity, however, is tempered by the fact that many of the previously anointed 'best trained, most dedicated, best whatever' stock of teachers are creating an impediment to progress by turning up for work in the morning.

In order to implement the 'Meet the new teacher, better than the old teacher' pogrom, they must first find 'justifiable' reason to dispense with the outmoded. And so we have mooted policy wearing the mask of creating a training 'entitlement' for teachers, the real intent of which is to drum the (say 15,000 or so) 'incompetent' teachers, as suggested by Chris Woodhead, out of employment. The sacrifice that such teachers will be forced into will serve the greater good. In having their careers laid down, they will create the space that superior successors might profitably populate. The issue with involuntary sacrifice, of course, is that no one ever stops to ask the lamb how it feels about having its throat cut, and in introducing a licence for teachers, the government plays the role of rabid high priest sharpening the knife.

Why, when there is already a thriving capability procedure routinely employed in many schools, is this considered necessary? In case you have not run into this, any teacher who consistently comes up with less than satisfactory observation grades, or whose classes' results have not vaulted sufficiently highly over the benchmark, all too quickly finds themselves subject to a series of accountability procedures, the intent of which is to either improve their performance sharpish or to make them leave the school. Anecdotally, those who fight this procedure tooth and nail tend to survive it. Most don't. After a brief, desperate and humiliating struggle, they recognise that leaving before they can be certified incapable is the better part of valour. If they leave before the capability procedure has reached a mature stage, they will be more likely to find another job; and so, they resign.

It is these teachers the government miscasts in the role of cancerous blight, and the licence to teach scheme is the operation designed to surgically remove them. But while it would be churlish to ignore the fact that there are probably more than a few teachers unsuited to the job, the collateral damage of this scheme will be awesome. Schools are all different. A certain type of teacher may well be shocking in one environment, perfectly successful in another. The licence to teach scheme suggests that such teachers, rather than finding a school environment in which they might thrive, should only have one strike before being not only out but permanently retired.

Furthermore, its invention raises a legion of operational questions. How will it map with capability procedures? Is it intended that all capabilities should, after the trial period, automatically become 'licence to teach' issues? And why, in the name of Beelzebub, trial it on the newly qualified? This is a vicious and self-defeating madness. Where a decade ago an NQT would be assigned a classroom and left to get on with it, learning on the job, the new breed will be allowed less room to make the mistakes through which they'll find the method; a couple of whimsical observations and all the investment in training them will have been for nought. They'll be certified inadequate in their first term and promptly spat out. The irony here is that the first cohort of teachers to be subject to such draconianism will include the bankers, ICT specialists and 'quality' graduates the scheme seeks to make space for.

A further issue is how this impinges on the function of the General Teaching Council. The GTC seems, to many teachers, to exist solely to run disciplinary proceedings for gross professional misconduct, and to take a sum of money out of their pay packets each year. Unless the licence to teach scheme is run by the GTC, does it not, in some way, obviate its existence?[17] Also, if the cutting out of perceived deadwood is now the responsibility of the head teacher, then who checks the head teacher's judgement?

The licence to teach is an ill-thought-out and vastly costly step that, if applied, will cut out the wrongly diagnosed cancer of the committed journeyman pro in favour of the unemployed financial services clerk. We will, I predict, come the recovery, have to get down on our knees and beg for them to be reinstated the moment, three years in, when the bankers realise en masse that teaching is far from the dossy, permanently uplifting stroll they had been sold by the glossy brochures and adverts.

Early Years Foundation Stage

All my sons are named after people who can't sing. My youngest, Lou Beadle, bears the same name as the surly, tuneless old rocker Lou Reed. He is 3½, though will insist he's 'nearly 4', and sports a shock of curly, ginger hair that, when combined with a facsimile version of his father's unfortunate nose, gives him the bearing of a miniature Crusty the Clown. Recently, much to my concern, he has taken, when enraged by some perceived unfairness, to calling me a 'bloody-hell-idiot!' He is a perceptive and intelligent boy.

Lou will tell you in fevered tones that he is 'a big boy now', but as much as I respect his opinion on things, well, he's not really. I'm not saying that he's lying, but when he gets upset, which is often, he'll put his right index finger into his mouth and tuck the top of his left ear in on itself, then

---

[17] It did. The GTC is no more.

rock himself gently. This – let's be honest – is no way to behave in the boardroom, and I think we will leave it for a while before we start grooming him as a future captain of industry.

We have been lucky with Lou, being relatively late starters to parenthood and hippies to boot. Mrs Beadle and I have managed to manoeuvre ourselves into a situation where, rather than buy into Britain's expanding culture of workaholism, we prioritise time at home with the kids; consequently, Lou is always looked after by either his Mum or his Dad. He hasn't had to go to nursery yet, and has never been looked after by someone upon whose cheek he wouldn't be comfortable bestowing an open mouthed, dribble kiss.

Notwithstanding our failure to properly engage Lou into the hurly-burly of preschool competition, we are relatively happy with his meagre academic attainment so far. Key achievements have been spotting Wally in the *Where's Wally?*, doing a bit of slightly haphazard counting and occasionally taking his pants to the dirty washing basket when he has had one of his increasingly rare accidents. When he finally does go to nursery, however, I'd like him to do the stuff he is good at: playing, jumping, dancing and making entirely inappropriate older women think he is cute.

The Statutory Framework for the Early Years Foundation Stage Goals has me worried for poor Lou, though. I suspect that, according to the government's Early Learning Goals, he may already be a significant underachiever and, when he finally gets to nursery, they will have him swiftly recorded on a register of children who are already deemed failures, and are at risk of becoming poly drug-addicted crazies.

Of the 69 separate targets he is to be assessed on over the next year and a half, there are many that may be beyond him. He is to write 'phonetically plausible attempts at more complex words' which, given at the moment he thinks pens are good for sucking and poking, I think he may fail. He is 'to write stories and instructions' – 'Dear Dad, get my dinner now (you bloody-hell-idiot)' – all of which are to be punctuated, 'with some consistency'. In terms of numeracy, he is expected to be fluent in concepts of quantity, 'more' or 'less', 'greater' or 'smaller'; perhaps even going as far as mastering the 'less' and 'fewer' conundrum that remains resolutely beyond his poor, innumerate Dad.

He is also to use 'information and communication technology and programmable toys to support her/his learning', despite the fact that such technology, with its flashing lights and bright colours, is bound to divert him from the books we keep shoving under his nose, and in the direction of computer games that will decimate his attention span and teach him that shooting people who disagree with him is normal behaviour.

In all honesty, the framework comes from a good place. Its intent being to narrow the class-based disparity in achievement that appears so early and is never closed. It is admirable that the government is seeking to address this. However, in making the framework statutory, it puts early years providers under the OFSTED driven pressures that have so narrowed the learning on offer to year six and year nine students.

The same curse as afflicts primary and secondary education will be visited on toddlers: providers will be forced to spend so much time proving that they are doing the job that it will reduce the time available to actually do it. Rather than teaching, looking after, keeping secure, giving kids a gentle introduction to formally organised environments, playing, running and jumping, nursery education will be provided by ladies with half an eye on the class and half an eye on a clipboard; a clipboard that will nag them into bouts of feverish ticking, when they could be dispensing a kind word, a fantastic piece of papier-mâché or a much-needed cuddle. And how much longer, I wonder, given our government's eagerness to ensure future generations are in a position to compete with emerging economies, before there is a Pre-Early Years Stage, where, with the use of a gynaecological version of an ear trumpet, midwives are required to take future school students through prenatal phonics drills? Careful now.

What is Personalisation?

My Dad has a retort when overburdened, which I can recommend teachers employ at the moment exactly one second after a member of senior management asks any question beginning with the phrase, 'Could you just ...?' Its use is limited to once a term to maintain its freshness and therefore its impact. It is, 'Why don't you shove a broom up my arse? I'll sweep the floor while I'm at it!'

I attended a seminar a couple of months ago at the Institute of Education, in which a representative of the GTC went through their response to the government's plans for personalised learning in schools. In amongst the colloquiums in search of consensus (que?) the one solid thing I took home (aside from a stolen bread roll) was the knowledge that personalised learning was not actually a concrete concept, but is actually an agenda. Ah. At last. Progress. But what kind of agenda? To clarify: it is not so much the kind of agenda you might use to order points for discussion, nothing so near to the realms of logic. It is more of an agenda in that you have to attach the prefix 'shadowy' to it before it reveals its true meaning.

The GTC suggested that personalised learning has been an agenda for debate. A debate that has excluded teachers and which seems to have gone:

DfES: Do what you're told.

Teaching Profession: What if I can prove there is no point in doing what I'm told?

DfES: Do what you're told.

The translation of ill-defined (to the point of undefined) rhetoric will always meet with problems in its translation into action. There are 'operational issues' with personalised learning; the kind of which you will always get if you attempt to push a slug through the eye of a needle. There is even the hint, conspiracy theorists, that the enormous delay in defining what personalised learning actually means was deliberate; it is so vaporous as to mean anything. Any policy feint can realistically be shimmied through on the basis that it is part of the personalisation agenda.

David Halpin, Professor of Education at the Institute of Education, has been pleasingly scathing about personalised learning. 'It is a typical New Labour "rubber bag" kind of expression into which almost anything can be fitted. By allowing for so much, it ultimately signifies very little of consequence or substance.'

Is Halpin right? A look at the Standards Site reveals that, following the debate, there are now five key components of personalised learning: four of which I recall being in receipt of as a schoolboy in the 1970s. Yes, the radicalism of personalised learning is really that profound!

'Assessment for Learning' is merely an over-wordy piece of jargon for 'mark their books to see what they need to learn next'. The component of 'Effective Teaching and Learning' – Gawd 'elp us – is already the key priority for every school in the world. 'Organising the School' instructs teachers that they should use 'displays to celebrate achievement'. Yawn. While 'Beyond the Classroom' is the usual tired blackmail that says teachers who dare to prioritise time at home with their own families are unprofessional and should be ashamed of themselves. It is, as former head teacher Andrea Berkeley rightly points out, 'The Martini curriculum – anytime, anywhere, any place.'

The staggering vacuity of this agglomeration of non-ideas is made all the more shocking when you think of how much taxpayers' money has been wasted for hordes of consultants and other vampiric tics to grow bloated with blood from the personalisation shekel. Money they have received for drawing conclusions on education that probably every single teacher in the post-war period could have come to after two days' experience.

It leads one to the conclusion that Professor Halpin is bang on the nose, and that all the personalised learning agenda ever was, was a sophisticated diversionary tactic. A diversionary tactic which he suggests has deliberately 'deflected attention away from awkward and highly ideologically inflected debate in education about which kids get what and under what circumstances'. Such as, for instance, why city academies are allowed to manipulate their admissions procedures so that only very few children from the estates they were meant to serve are allowed to go there.

However, in amongst the four non-ideas nestles the component 'Curriculum Entitlement and Choice' which states: 'Where the National Curriculum is not the most appropriate route to maximising pupils' learning and achievement, disapplication of all, or parts of, the curriculum can occur.' This appears a fairly revolutionary statement hidden amongst the dross, and was expanded last week by Ken Boston of the Qualifications and Curriculum Authority, so that now a quarter of the time in secondary schools need not be spent on the National Curriculum. This strikes many as a radical and overdue initiative, freeing schools to set their own curriculum, which is responsive to the needs of their students. However, there is another way of looking at it. It may be merely a covert means of allowing the many and increasing business academies or schools with a notional specialism in Business and Enterprise to introduce five-year courses in filing and tea making. It needs further explanation.

I am left with the overriding feeling that with the personalisation issue the DfES has, once again, assumed the role of the Chelsea manager before Mourinho. His name was Claudio Ranieri, the Tinkerman. He fiddled around a bit, won nothing. The result of the personalised learning agendas, when it finally reaches the classroom is, as I predicted last year, that it will be a whip with which to force teachers to differentiate by task for every single lesson taught, and that they will be employing my dear old Dad's phrase far, far, more often than just once a term.

Religious Studies

I spent the summer holiday in a villa on the Algarve, accompanied by Richard Dawkins, Christopher Hitchens and a staunchly Roman Catholic Mum. Dawkins and Hitchens, of course, came in my bag; Mum could not be convinced to join them.[18]

I've always imagined that questioning a pupil's inherited belief system in class was a sackable offence. I imagine this because I've never really had the guts to test it out, what with my own children needing shoes and stuff (though, that is not to say that I haven't been tempted). Kids' justifications of the religious beliefs inflicted upon them by various agencies usually hinge upon what sages describe as the 'Because it does. Right?' argument, and this renders the temptation to just apply the merest, tiniest, most wafer-thin pinpricks to their balloon quite awful.

Thankfully, for the English-teaching atheist, there's literature. You know the stuff ... written by great men ... (or women) ... full of superior insights ... generally satirical or scathing when dealing with what man will do in the name of faith. *The Crucible* has allowed me to allude to the hell that my pupils might experience should they ever attempt to employ their questioning spirits in a theocratic society. It is down to *Of Mice and Men* that I've been able to ask them to imagine the possibility that heaven might be a lie conjured up to keep them in their place, without the fear of a sacking.

---

[18] This is a joke. My mum is religious(ish), she doesn't buy atheism. I did not attempt to put my mother in a bag. I am pretending.

So, it was with some delight that I spent my summertime sweating with Christopher Hitchens in a pool of anti-theistic zeal next to a swimming pool in downtown Vilamoura.

Having gathered lots of fantastic facts – did you know, for instance, that the idea of Mary's assumption into heaven wasn't defined as holy dogma until 1950? – I resolved that my first column on returning would be to write a piece arguing that, since atheism now has its own version of the good book, perhaps it could now assume its place on the Religious Studies curriculum, and moreover, since religion is a pretty binary choice – you believe: you don't believe – perhaps it would be even handed to give half the curriculum time spent studying the various versions of idol worship to its more rational, analytical antithesis.

All sounds reasonable enough. Job done. But then I made the mistake of doing some research.

Two years ago Charles Clarke introduced the first ever 'non-statutory' framework for the teaching of religious education. In case you didn't know, kids have a legally protected 'entitlement' to Religious Studies, but there is no statutory control over what is taught. It is, for instance, entirely plausible that schools could teach children, without so much as a threat of a chastening governmental finger, that those children alone are God's elect, that faiths apart from the one they follow are entirely deluded and that it is entirely righteous to wage holy war on those who, by accident, are born on the other side of a wall to them. If I wanted to set up a Satanist school, and it's a thought I entertain from time to time, I could.

The framework itself, given that it had to accommodate viewpoints as diverse as the Russian Orthodox Church and the British Union Conference of Seventh Day Adventists, pretty well all perspectives on religious education in fact (aside, of course, from those of the National Secular Society), is about as sane as these things can be. It is when we delve into the realms of suggested practice that it all gets a bit Old Testament.

The Standards Site features exemplar schemes of work for key stage three, which – some commendably tissue-thin sophistry aside – may as well have been written by Billy Graham. Creationism on the curriculum is not just happening in the American Bible Belt or in aberrant outposts on Teeside; the government recommends it as a topic for study in every school in the country. The suggested learning outcomes suggest that all year nine pupils should be able to 'explain the nature and meanings of the Genesis creation story for theists, creationists and others'. It goes on to state a desired intention that children 'understand that science leaves questions of ultimate meaning and purpose unanswered'.

There is a logical pedagogic link here that, though it may have been intended to promote a mature, dialectical approach to these themes, actually gives explicit permission and approval to those who want to teach creationism as fact. First, you teach the existence of the theory, then question science's ability to answer questions about our genesis.

The desired conclusion of this scheme of work is that children 'understand that historians of science now view the conflict account as misleading'. Let me unpack this disgracefully disingenuous phrase for you: the government's desired final outcome of Religious Studies teaching in

British schools is that children realise there is no conflict between religious belief and the evidence of science. This is a lie, the extent of which, so my catechism tells me, hits the three criteria for a mortal sin: it is grave, it is committed in full knowledge of the sin and it is deliberate.

It goes further. Having invigilated Religious Education exams before, and having had a shufty at the papers, I had always suspected that the mark schemes rewarded blind obedience to a theistic point of view: 'List ten reasons why God exists' (10 marks), 'Come up with a shaky reason he might not' (1 mark). These suspicions are finally confirmed with a look at the Standards Site's exemplar materials. The first scheme of work that is suggested for pupils on entry to secondary school is full of affirmations of the nature of religious truth and arguments for the existence of a deity. There ain't much there for the secularists to be singing about.

My father's generation had a timetabled lesson that went by the name of Religious Instruction, RI for short. There is a valid argument – though there is an equally valid and never-ventured argument for its abolition – that some form of religious education is vital for children to operate as decent members of a pluralist society. Where Religious Studies is of value is as a disinterested study of the customs of those people you are going to school with. As such, the only stakeholder group likely to produce Religious Studies materials with the appropriate degree of dispassion would, I think, be the National Secular Society.

As it is, the government's suggested framework gives schools explicit permission to reinstate RI, but this time the 'I' stands not for instruction, but for indoctrination and, things remaining so, Sir Peter Vardy receives his reward on earth (yet again). Blessed indeed are the automotive retailers!

Floor Targets and Secondary Moderns

Ed Balls's[19] announcement that those academies who don't hit the floor target of 30 percent of students gaining five A* to C grades by 2011 will be stripped of their sponsor can be taken as evidence of a gifted intellect, reaching out to the left of his party in anticipation of an imminent leadership contest; or, alternatively, a sign that educational policy has taken a lurch in a direction more surreal than a Jimmy Hendrix guitar solo on acid.

'What, Mr Balls, do we do when schools under local authority control fail to hit the floor target?'

'Well, we give them a sponsor of course. Sponsors are vital to the process of school improvement.'

'And how about when academies fail?'

'Well, surely it's obvious. We take the sponsor away. Importing expertise from (cough) private industry doesn't always work.'

'And if they fail once the sponsor has been taken away?'

'Well, we give them a sponsor of course. What are you? An idiot?'

Nestling 'neath the Minister's plans for 'sponsor hokey-cokey' come 2011, there's another announcement that catches the eye, and raises a fundamental question about

---

[19] In his time as Education Secretary I never once managed to pluck up the guts to refer to his middle name: Talks.

how the floor target affects different institutions. It is reported that the government intends, as part of National Challenge, to send in a crack team of advisors to schools in Kent, where there are concerns not enough is being done to hit the government's targets. Kent, as we know, has a system of selective education and hosts many of the 170 secondary modern schools in England.

Many of these schools have substantial challenges that may make hitting the floor target beyond them. Other National Challenge schools, in areas which do not have a selective system, are heavily reliant for a bedrock 20 percent of their A to Cs on the attainment of their top sets; children who, despite the fact that they may come from backgrounds distanced from being middle class, are both bright and motivated; children who will achieve results in whatever educational environment they find themselves. Under a selective system pretty well all these children are creamed off and placed into the grammars, leaving the secondary moderns without access to the cohort of kids for whom the attainment of the benchmark grades is relatively unproblematic. This means that a top set in a secondary modern is likely to mirror the attainment profile of what is now called an intervention set (the C/D borderlines) everywhere else.

Furthermore, secondary moderns have to deal every year with an intake of seriously depressed young people who already regard themselves as failures. I heard tell last week of a teacher from a secondary modern who, on being introduced to a 10-year-old about to go through the Eleven plus exam, was asked by the child whether she taught at a 'pass' school or a 'fail' school. The fact that most secondary moderns take a set of kids already labelled with failure, all of whom will require substantial intervention to reach the benchmark, and not only set about rebuilding their charges' shattered sense of self-worth, but in many cases achieve substantially more than the floor target, is evidence that the teachers in many secondary moderns are doing fantastically against the odds.

There is, I think, a reasonable question to be levied at government regarding the place of 40 percent of the country's secondary moderns in the National Challenge, and it is this: given that the children who walk through their doors every September already have an attainment profile radically downshifted from those who enter a comprehensive should they not be judged against a different floor target?

We are all aware of the Labour Party's educational mantra: 'Poverty is not an excuse.' (Which, of course, is right. Poverty is not an excuse. It is a condition. The dog ate my homework is an excuse.) But, in insisting that secondary moderns adhere to the same floor target as comprehensives, they extend the mantra to implicitly include the markedly less catchy, 'Previously low attainment and being labelled a failure is no excuse either.'

The DCSF, perhaps in anticipation of objections to secondary moderns having, notionally at least, the same floor target as the grammar schools alongside them, seem hip to the unfairness of this equation; and have previously announced preferential weighting in funding to non-selective schools in selective areas. Secondary moderns in particularly problematic circumstances receive up to £250,000 additional money from the National Challenge over three years. They must also be applauded on the fact that the National Challenge is an enormously valuable and right-thinking programme. Whilst some head teachers have found the resulting headlines in the regional press of 'Local School to Close' unhelpful, it unarguably directs funding to those schools that most need it. And besides, isn't it only right that government attempts an aspirational guarantee of minimum expected attainment for all schools?

A look at the stats suggests that its precursor, London Challenge, has been extremely successful in raising attainment: of the nine regions London has the third lowest percentage of schools in the National Challenge, only 17 percent. A further look, though, shows that the three counties with most schools attaining below 30 percent five A* to C are Kent (33), Birmingham (27) and Lincolnshire (18). What do these counties have in common? They operate a selective system – completely in Lincolnshire and Kent, partially in Birmingham.

Ed Balls has been pleasingly open about the fact that he is no great fan of selection, but has always backed this up with the caveat that he accepts that 'Selection is a local decision for parents and local authorities.' It is a shame that there is no political will to make this the national decision it should be. Accepting that the teachers in secondary modern schools are perhaps the most admirable of all, and that many schools succeed brilliantly against the odds, wouldn't Mr Balls's brilliantly subversive suggestion of a merger between grammars and secondary moderns give these three counties a chance, at least, of having a less conspicuously high number of their schools attaining results that are far enough below the floor as to suggest the counties consider investing in a basement conversion?

Importing the Private Sector

Near enough every adult in British society went to school at some point, and they all have opinions on how they should be run. I have yet to meet a cab driver who, on hearing I was a teacher, wasn't able to tell me, in detail, exactly what I was doing wrong.

Other professionals don't have to endure this particular torment. Teachers do not think they know how to run the health service, but there will be a proportion of doctors who think they know how to run schools; likewise, a majority of economists, a proportion of accountants, many used-car salesmen, drug dealers and footballers. But there is a difference between having an opinion and having one worth listening to. I have opinions about the correct deployment of Frank Lampard, but I'd be disappointed if Sven took them into account.

With the Education Bill passing its third reading there will now be ever more opportunities for the private sector to force their expertise onto our schools. One wonders why they'd want to do so.

Price Waterhouse's 2003 Academies Evaluation for the DfES lists three main motivations for educational sponsorship: commerce, gift and 'returnship'. The commercial motivation, whereby children attending sponsored schools are seen as potential consumers to be indoctrinated into the company mindset is surely too nakedly Orwellian to be allowed to happen, and the gift motivation is acknowledged by the authors of the report as being 'small-scale'. 'Returnship' is where the sponsor seeks to 'give something back'. Schools will import the patronage of those who, having realised the depths of their previous thoughtlessness, now seek redemption by masquerading a previously uncharacteristic ambition to help others.

One of Mr Blair's policy advisors told me recently that more or less every study ever undertaken shows that importing principles and people from private industry vastly improves public services. It has not been spelled out to education professionals how they do this: what do they bring to the table apart from lucre and questionable intent?

A 'think piece' document available from the DfES Innovation Unit gives us some indication. *Innovation: Lessons from the Private Sector* tells of innovation factories, knowledge-brokering cycles and processes that are 'rational, non-destructive and manufacturer led'. From this it seems that what private sector involvement brings is a soaking from a bucket full of linguistic crud.

The issue with importing the views of the private sector into the expert, professional realm of the trained educator is not so much with the structures they might implement, but with the fact that they know nothing about our core business, teaching. Flogging a used car is poor preparation for involvement in the infinitely more sophisticated and more important process of educating a generation of children. The motivations to educate and to turn a profit are so dissimilar as to be antithetical; bean counters may have issues in determining where the profit is in strong special needs provision, when they could be employing more marketing staff.

I have worked in both sectors, alongside some of the accountancy firms who are queuing up for the new markets education might provide. And before joining the profession I was in possession of some of the prejudices redolent in the private sector. But until you've seen how hard something is from the inside, then you, like the infinite number of cab drivers who've given me advice, have little moral right to assume an authoritative position on it.

The arguments and ideas of Blair's advisor were based on studies of the American version of the health service: a service not much enjoyed by those who live on welfare support. These ideas have become the basis of the now pre-ferred model of schooling in this country, and they do not preclude the eventual full privatisation of British schools.

So when Alan Johnson says, 'We must push ahead with a refreshed and revitalised radicalism in our schools policy,' you have every reason to be afraid. They haven't finished yet. Not by a long chalk.

The Myth of the Failing School

When was the last time you saw the Deputy Editor of *The Times* in your school assembly? Is a senior member of the editorial staff of the *Evening Standard* perhaps moonlight-ing as a learning support assistant? Maybe a leader writer from *The Telegraph* pops in to supplement his wage with a bit of occasional supply work?

There's been a lot of opinion expressed about the govern-ment's plans for education reform: editorials written by (senior) journalists. Many of these journalists will have reached the government's required standards of literacy; some may even have been to a parents' evening. None, how-ever, are remotely cognisant with the day-to-day demands of running a school.

If they had any first-hand, 'adult' experience of education they would not so easily perpetuate the fundamental lie on which much of the recent support for the government's plans appears to be based: that of the 'failing' school.

For them, the existence of this mythical beast is the irrefutable evidence of the need for a shake-up of our educational institutions; the 'failing' school is an opinion which, repeated often enough, has taken on the tenor of fact.

For those who work in such schools – schools more often than not found serving the less well-off communities (in OFSTED's last list there were three 'failing' secondary schools in Salford, three in Bradford, none in Berkshire) – it is a counterproductive label which devalues a whole community, and casts a mortal professional slur on the teachers who choose to work there.

Let there be no doubt about this, if any of the commentators visited the 'failing' schools they so deride, they would find pockets of astonishing success: astounding individuals, teachers and students, indefatigable spirit, creative brilliance. Teachers working in such schools are often the finest our profession has to offer; the chaos, lawlessness and lack of rigour painted in the leader writers' columns does not exist.

There has been a shift in the tone of these editorials since the cessation of low hysteria and common bloodlust surrounding the sex offenders' register. The measures are now not radical enough! This shift has coincided with the publication of GCSE results showing their biggest rise in the last decade. Somehow, elements of the press have twisted this success story so that what it actually shows is that standards in English and maths (which have both risen) have reached the point of national catastrophe.

This fictionalised catastrophe is used, along with the fantasy of school failure, to portray our schools as creaking catastrophes ready for the knacker's yard, and to justify a move forward into what appears to me a pre-industrial future; a future in which educational provision is (again) the province of sectarian religious groups, benevolent industrialists and spurious 'charitable' institutions. Messrs Blair and Adonis, both graduates of private schooling, appear to assume that the version of education they received as children should be rolled out across the country as, to quote the father taking a belt to his child, 'It never did me any harm.'

Anyone who objects to this exercise in de-evolution is painted an enemy of progress. But making our schools socially divided, unregulated and factionalised competitors scrabbling for high ability students is not progress.

Progress is this: in 1970, 47 percent of pupils left secondary school with no qualifications; in 2005 that figure was down to 4 percent. This is the result of a largely comprehensive system that has worked, and is working. State governed comprehensive schools have increased the potential of upward social mobility for all. I write as the recipient of such an education, the son of a lorry driver churning out words in a broadsheet newspaper.

Mr Blair has presided over many improvements during his reign, but as William Atkinson wrote in his sparklingly eloquent piece in *Education Guardian*, 'The government is creating a false picture of education as a basket case.'

It is never good to believe your own PR, but this is an area where Mr Blair should really take a look at his achievements, congratulate himself and then think what a shame it would be to spoil it all in the final moments.

Private Schools

There is a wood on a hillside in south-east London. It is set in 60 acres of scrupulously kept playing fields. Hidden away amongst the two full-size AstroTurf pitches, one practice pitch, an athletics track, twelve rugby pitches, ten football pitches, ten cricket squares and nine tennis courts, there also nestles one scruffy and solitary municipal football ground.

You have to pay a toll to gain access to College Road, Dulwich. Once this has been negotiated a child might fantasise about what it would be like to play in the woods or on those fields. But they would remain fantasies, because these 60 acres are reserved for the children of the rich. Local children have to content themselves with the one scrappy football pitch.

Anthony Seldon, the Master of Wellington College, recently suggested, 'The ritual denigration of independent schools has got to end. It is a 20th-century discourse, and its time has passed.'

Mr Seldon is a unique man, but surely while equality of educational opportunity remains an aspiration for the future, the dialogue about whether these bastions of privilege continue to uphold and promote societal division must remain current.

The ideological arguments about the continued existence (or not) of these organisations are well rehearsed, but worth repeating. Only 7 percent of our children attend such institutions, yet somehow they account for 44 percent of students going to Oxbridge. Independent schools maintain the right to rule of a privileged elite. And they are extremely successful in doing so. Eton, as Auberon Waugh said, is very good at getting stupid boys into parliament!

But being successful at something when that something causes damage to the fabric of society doesn't mean you should be allowed to continue. As an example, here are the thoughts of Jonathan Shephard, Head of the Independent Schools Council (ISC) on selection in schools. In a leaked report, *A Cold Look at the Independent Sector* issued on 14th September last year, he states, 'Government opposition to selection frustrates social mobility by tying children to their immediate environment. This is morally wrong and educationally ineffective.'

The fact that a senior representative of the independent sector describes a move towards equality of opportunity for children in pejorative moral terms shows why they would want to keep any argument in the previous century. Because that's where arguments for such institutionalised inequality belong, the – sadly, not too distant – past.

But the British ruling class and their institutions are nothing if not adaptable. In order to maintain their grotesque and undeserved charitable status many are deigning to enter into some form of tokenistic partnership with state institutions. Jonathan Shephard himself writes about widening access: 'We would be delighted to get children from the disadvantaged areas ... And if it was only 20 into each of our schools, that is 24,000 children who are saved, in fact, from what might be a very bad education.'

The messianic tone in this statement is somewhat undermined by the wilful ignorance of standards of education in such disadvantaged areas. Any state school entering into partnership should be careful they are not being made an Uncle Tom. The ISC website says, '90% of ISC schools make at least one facility available to outside use'. Phew! At least one? (Sometimes even up to two?) This statement goes somewhere towards illustrating the shameful extent of their attempts to prove they are of public benefit.

I am not suggesting that the playing fields of Eton be dug up and the buildings bulldozed. There is a better solution, which is admittedly at odds with the prevailing view of the future of education in government. What better way to avoid the accusations of tokenism and elitism, to ensure these historical institutions remain of service to the public and to preserve some beautiful buildings, but to slap them under LEA control and turn them all into comprehensives.

There are 74 different pitches and courts at Dulwich College, a gymnasium and a swimming pool. It would be nice if local children could use more than one of them.

The Epidemic of Homophobia

Leafing through boys' achievement expert, Gary Wilson's, *Help your Boys Succeed*, I've chanced upon a horrifying statistic that suggests we are in the midst of a national crisis that almost no one knows about.

Wilson refers to statistics presented in the brilliantly titled document, *Stand Up For Us – Challenging Homophobia in School*, released as part of the Health Schools initiative, and the passage he quotes is shocking. As an introduction, a study undertaken by Professors Ian Rivers and Helen Cowie in 2001 suggests that 85 percent of lesbian, gay and bisexual (LGB) men and women experienced some form of homophobic bullying at school. The document goes on to state that, 'Another UK study found that more than 50 percent of LGB men and women who had been bullied at school contemplated self-harm or suicide, while 40 percent had made at least one attempt to self-harm. A further study found that more than 20 percent had attempted suicide.'

More or less all LGB children suffer homophobic bullying in our schools, and one in five of those attempt suicide! These figures stand as formal testimony to a hidden issue that I've witnessed, day to day, over the space of many years: British schools are the final, blithe bastions of homophobia, which is, and has always been, at epidemic proportions in them. In schools where racism is unheard of and sexism is petering out, protecting the rights of gay children to their identity being accepted is perceived within our school system as an equality too far. Homophobia, in British schools, is the last remaining acceptable prejudice.

This appalling state of affairs is, as one might predict, all the worse in faith schools. Stonewall's report on the same subject lists that while 65 percent of pupils in non-denominational schools have experienced homophobic bullying, this rises to 75 percent in faith schools. Students experiencing such bullying in faith school are also far less likely to report it.

Homophobia in schools is an intolerance that had, until five years ago, government backing, in the form of the loathsome Section 28, which, though it was claimed didn't actually apply to schools, was a direction to all local authorities that they should not 'promote the teaching in any maintained school of the acceptability of homosexuality as a pretended family relationship'.

I remember being determined on entering the profession that I would, at some point, teach children the acceptability of homosexuality as a normal lifestyle. And it occurred to me that the oddly worded Section 28 wouldn't stop me from doing so. Its function, so it appeared, was to stop the local authority telling me to promote homosexual partnerships as 'pretend' families; as such it was fine for me, an individual teacher, to suggest they could be 'real' families. Also, the idea of any teacher promoting homosexuality is absurd. Teachers are not advertising executives for any one sexual preference. Section 28 was a knee-jerk sop to the moral majority inflamed by an article in the *Daily Mail* about the book, *Jenny Lives with Eric and Martin* being found in a school library.

But in caving in and making preposterous laws, the government of the time sent a message to the education world, that is: speaking up in schools for the rights of LGB people is dangerous ground for any teacher to decide to stand upon. The fact that this prevails in 2008, five years after Section 28 was thrown in the dumper where it belongs, should be a matter for deep and intense national shame.

In British schools thousands of our gay and lesbian colleagues – mature, intelligent, professional, respectable adults – are wary of being, erm, straight with the children they teach about who exactly they are. This awful code of enforced secrecy transmits to the children, so that young people facing up to the fact that they might not be exactly what their parents had in mind are forced to suffer the existential agonies of doubt in silence, unaware the role model they desperately need, and think is absent, is actually standing at the front of the very class in which they are suffering. Those who don't maintain the code of silence risk being publicly tarred and feathered at breaktime.

What solution then? The *Stand Up For Us* document lists audits, bullying forms and links to resources that don't exist. It is a worthy and enlightened document, but the issue is one of visuality. Gary Wilson talks of the need to inculcate in young males a vision of caring maleness, so that what the gender theorists refer to as hegemonic masculinity, and others will know as grunt culture, is not the only option open to boys.

I have taken this to mean that it is imperative that we teach children that certain 'deviant' paths are, in fact, perfectly desirable, in that they are not as blankly anti-achievement as hegemonic masculinity. Consequently, the display board entitled 'acceptable versions of masculinity' in my class features pictures of billionaire geeks; cross-dressing athletes; transvestite comedians; disabled, Irish, punk shouters; transsexual models; gay, black activists; lesbian singers; goths; and (reputedly) gay footballers.

This display has been the springboard for much discussion. The kids like it, do not, under any circumstances, want it taken down and enjoy having a chance to discuss the issues it brings up. It also gives me the chance to promote the acceptability of homosexuality as a normal lifestyle.

And there is a lesson for all teachers. If we are to avoid a significant percentage of our children being victimised, leading into self-hatred, self-harm and suicide attempts, then we should, in direct opposition to the spirit of Section 28, be teaching homosexuality as something that it is perfectly reasonable to be.

I have today ordered a copy of *Jenny Lives with Eric and Martin* for the school library and shall be using it in lessons as soon as it arrives, and I'll do this with the full support of the boss. The school I work for, Oasis Academy Coulsdon, is run by a Christian organisation, whose head, the Rev. Steve Chalke, has recently been quoted in *Education Guardian* as saying, 'You can either be a Christian school or a school for

Christians. You can't be both.' As a Christian, Rev. Chalke is happy for Oasis, as a faith-based organisation, to be publicly and explicitly against any form of homophobia in its schools.

Would it be too much to ask that other faith-based organisations in British education are able to follow his lead on this publicly, so that the LGB children who most certainly attend their schools feel sufficiently empowered to report such bullying before it ends in self-harm and suicide attempts? Or is this repulsive status quo still, in certain cabals, perceived as entirely acceptable in the 21st century?

Trans Kids

Ego surfing when you have some pitiful, public micro-profile is a bit of a Pandora's box. Ordinarily, however, those who make contributions to the *Guardian*'s site can be relied upon for a pretty measured and intelligent standard of comment. Unlike some of the other education forums, you don't feel as if you have to take a wash after visiting the *Guardian* site. I'll sometimes read through them, either nodding sagely in agreement or shaking my curls emitting a wild, cockney cry of 'Nahmateyougotthatallwrong.'

Last month, however, one comment got more than a cursory gesture or utterance. It humbled me. 'Natacha' wrote so movingly of the challenge facing transgendered children in our schools, that I feel it's only right to make a public apology and to address the issue. If the human rights of LGB children in our schools are, as I wrote last month, routinely ignored, then the rights of transgendered children are not even recognised as existing.

I contacted Natacha, who I now know as Natacha Kennedy, a former primary schoolteacher who is transgender and has researched widely into the issue. What she has to say about how our schools treat the issue screams to be shared.

First some detail. According to Debra Davis, Executive Director of the Gender Education Center in the USA, gender is only simple, 'if you're an earthworm'. Transgenderism is a catch-all term that, broadly, encompasses anyone whose gender identity does not unambiguously match that which they have been assigned. Transgendered does not automatically mean transsexual. The vast majority (95 percent) live in the role of the gender other than that which they have been assigned, without ever considering gender reassignment surgery; but the fact that the average age of someone choosing such surgery has been, consistently, and for some time, 42 years of age suggests that many spend a substantial proportion of their adult lives suppressing their transgenderism.

Since many people keep their transgenderism entirely hidden it is difficult to accurately assess how many people live their lives this way, but best guesses hover around an estimate that around 1 percent of the population are transgendered, which is roughly the equivalent of the population of, say, Sheffield.

This would mean that in a large, British secondary school as many as ten or so kids could be transgender. Their lives, reports Natacha, can be awesomely difficult. Whereas LGB children may come to a realised understanding of their difference post puberty, transgendered children often come to this awareness before they are 8 years of age.

'Bullying of transgendered children is utterly vicious and is completely ingrained in our culture,' says Natacha. The comedy transvestite, for instance, is an intrinsic part of British comic culture and is so popular a stereotype that it renders bullying of transgender people almost a compulsory, cultural obligation.

And what is the result of such bullying? Unhappiness, loneliness and suicide attempts. A spokesperson from the organisation Mermaids, which provides support to children and families dealing with transgender issues, has said that 'A number of our children have made attempts on their own lives, thankfully unsuccessful.' However, in Doncaster, last year, 10-year-old Cameron McWilliams, who had been asking permission to wear make-up and girls' underwear, hung himself.

'And still there is no effective recognition of the problems that transgendered children face,' Natacha reports. 'Most of them are aware they are transgendered for most, if not all their time in school. Most leave as soon as they can because the school system, whilst demanding that they show respect and tolerance for other minority groups, is utterly intolerant of transgenderism.

How then are schools to deal with this issue? Should there be compulsory gender studies as part of the citizenship curriculum? One would think so, but if kids are experiencing gender dysphoria at the age of 7, then it is the primary schools that must take a lead on this, well before the nightmare that transgendered children experience as puberty begins.

Natacha's feeling is that schools should, at an early age, be looking at notions of gender identity, and that this could help alleviate some of the feelings of guilt and shame which will traumatise some transgendered children. 'What transgendered children need is for their teachers to talk to their classes about transgenderism and its problems, even if there may not be a transgendered child in the class. Those that are in the classes need to know that they are OK. They are not freaks. They have rights. And there are many others like them.'

So, in clarification of my claim last month that homophobia in British schools is the last acceptable prejudice: transphobia remains an inequality enshrined in law. The government is proposing to exclude the majority of transgendered people from any protection against discrimination in the Equality Bill, as they say that transgendered people 'choose' to live the way they do and there is no evidence of any systemic discrimination. Both of which, according to Natacha, are wrong. It is still legal to discriminate against transgendered people in situations where racism, homophobia, sexism, Islamophobia and disability discrimination are outlawed.

This is an area that the DCSF needs to take a serious look at. They have been farsighted and enlightened in producing materials and documents guiding schools in how to deal with issues surrounding homophobic bullying. But, given their lead on this, and the Labour Government's excellent record in dealing with equalities issues, it is time that they took action to eliminate what is indeed the very, very last acceptable prejudice.[20]

---

[20] Natacha Kennedy has set up a website to aid teachers who want advice and support about this issue: http://transkids. synthasite.com

Drugs

The good burghers of Faversham have plenty of reasons to be proud. It's been voted best market town in Kent, and in 2005 it was even listed in the top three for the whole of the South East region. Of the 'things to do' listed on the town's website there's outdoor Shakespeare, a medieval pageant and Cherry Week. Markedly absent from the recommendations however is the option of hanging around the market square scoring rocks of crack from a toothless fellow addict.

Now I'm aware that, should this pastime exist in the leafiest part of the garden of England, then it's unlikely to be publicised on its website, but I suspect that – at least compared to the inner cities – Faversham does not have a significant drug problem.

Why then did former head teacher of the Abbey School in Faversham, Peter Walker, seek to get his name plastered all over the newspapers by introducing drugs testing at his school? (The answer here is cunningly secreted in the question.)

This happened last year, and Mr Walker proclaimed the experiment such a success that he attributed the school's 10 percent rise in five A to C passes to it. But hold on for a second. Can introducing drugs testing at a school improve results? Surely, finding such a causal link is little more than crack-head logic. A 10 percent rise in A to C grades may reasonably be attributed to improvements in the teaching at the school, to a particularly good cohort of students or even to their relief at the impending retirement of a manically punitive, publicity-seeking head teacher. It cannot be solely attributable to infringing the human rights of students, or to creating a climate of petrified obeisance amongst schoolchildren.

The story was snapped up by the red tops, and Peter Walker now continues his good work (post-retirement) as the ambassador for the programme now being rolled out all over Kent. He is happy to provide advice to other head teachers wishing to criminalise the children in their own schools.

I'd like to raise a hand in fierce protest here. Random drugs testing in schools necessarily means that 11-year-old children will be forced into a line-up in which they must see themselves as being potentially criminal. The paltry and expedient lip service to the Human Rights Act that the testing is voluntary cuts little muster. Schools create a climate in which obedience is required and only one in seven children at the Abbey School found the strength of character to stand up for their human rights and refuse the test. Not a large cohort. And one can imagine that their spirited refusal to submit themselves to such an invasion might give the school reason to conclude they are doing so because they are drug users. The school might then argue a case for calling in the constabulary, who have the right to enforce a drugs test.

The human rights organisation, Liberty, describes this as a 'worrying trend in which children are treated as criminals without the need for any evidence'. They also raise the worry that, 'A child who opts out will almost certainly become suspect.'

Much of government policy in schools is about imposing – and moreover being seen to impose – control on that handy scapegoat, youth. Witness the repulsive and reductive dogma of 'zero tolerance'. Making our own children enemies for an utterly wrong-headed agenda that relies on the lowest order of retrograde puritanism is unforgivable.

Should the experiment in Kent be proclaimed responsible for the rise in GCSE passes, which would be achieved more easily by scrapping the grammar school system to which they cling, then you can bet drugs testing will be considered by more LEAs. Should it come to your town, see it for what it is: random drugs testing is child abuse; it should be stopped.

Peter Walker has been treated as a heroic revolutionary in some quarters. Quarters in which heroism can achieved by appealing to the ignorant prurience of the lowest common denominator of public opinion rather than standing resolute by Abbey School's motto, which is, somewhat ironically, 'Respecting each other as individuals'.

Class

Vocational Learning

Kelsey Park School for Boys wasn't called that for nothing: it was opposite Kelsey Park, and there weren't any girls there. It isn't called that any more though. It is now Kelsey Park Sports College; and features a blossoming football academy, undergraduates of which are currently spanking other school teams countrywide.

I went to 'Kelsey' (as it is known amongst the alumni who gather at the Coach and Horses to lament their passing into middle age) as a boy, leaving with a rudimentary grasp of basic Marxist tenets, a lifelong interest in T. S. Eliot, some O and A levels and a CSE grade 2 in drama.

Though the school is situated in one of the richest streets you could conceive of, its catchment is predominantly drawn from the markedly less salubrious Penge. Penge, which is pronounced Pénge by the few aspirant residents with sufficient detachment from reality to believe social mobility still exists, has had few notable residents, unless one counts irritating DJ, Pat Sharp, and famous plumber, Sir Thomas Crapper, as being, respectively, the 'great' and the 'good'. It is also where I spent the first 19 years of my life. Penge is the last mouldering wound on London's fair city, before it dissolves into the, perhaps scarier, white ghettos of suburban Bromley. Despite its SE20 postcode, Penge has many of the indices of the inner city and, like Sharpy, Sir Thomas and myself, its residents can be a pretty rum bunch.

Socially, Bromley, aside from Penge on the London side and the Kray twins (St Mary's and Foot's) on the Kent side, is wealthy. Its schools are extremely successful; and it is testament to how phenomenally well Kelsey Park School is doing (80 percent of boys leaving the sixth form gaining entry to the university of their choice) that it manages to keep up with its snootier neighbours, despite the catchment it serves.

I went there recently, sitting nervously outside the head's office waiting to be summoned. The last time I had sat in that spot was 25 years ago, and I was in serious trouble. As one of the so-called 'dirty half-dozen', whose bad works were orchestrated by a boy called Simon 'Mac Vicar' Lloyd, I'd been accused and convicted of several acts of wanton immaturity. Twenty-five years on, I wait outside the same office, to meet a man bearing the same job title as the person I was to meet a quarter of a century ago. This time, however, the head teacher, Brian Lloyd (no relation to Simon), didn't ban me from the sixth form social accommodation for six months; he showed me around the school and talked through his plans for it.

It's an odd experience going round your old school, meeting the one member of staff who was there when you were at school (no, he didn't remember me) and observing that the building, which had something of a prefabricated feel in the 1970s, is exactly the same. There has been the odd add-on – a new drama class has been ingeniously suspended above the school hall and a whole new wing has been built – but the classrooms in which my fledgling love of words was ignited and validated are the same. The most striking differences are in the energy of the head teacher and the fact that he has employed a full-time gardener, so the boys are surrounded by the civilising and beautifying influence of extravagant flora.

And it is during my tour around the school and my acceptance of the head teacher's invite to speak at the leavers' bash next year in exchange for a 'substantially excellent' bottle of red, that something strikes me. Should there be such a thing as a regular reader of this column, they will have noticed one of my publishable passions is to highlight the fact that white working class kids are the forgotten mass. A recent correspondent, one Richard Birmingham, pinned the button directly on the pearly king suit, suggesting to me that the education system's attitude historically to white working class kids is that they will 'get the same jobs as their parents. Have access to the same healthcare and poor leisure resources'.

Walking around Kelsey Park Sports College with Mr Lloyd, it becomes apparent that this man has the most rational and best solution to some of the problems inherent in middle class institutions holding middle class aspirations up to working class children, and telling them that the only collar worth wearing is a white one.

Taking me to the sports hall, the bitumen floor of which has been staining kids' white trainers black for decades, he talks me through his plans for it. The head teacher wants to convert it into a Construction Technology Centre, where kids from the age of 13, who opt for it, will be taught the skills of bricklaying, carpentry, dry lining, painting, decorating and IT based CAD/CAM skills.

Potentially, what might this do for the boys at Kelsey Park Sports College who choose to supplement their academic work with hard, vocational skills? It will show them that the school values the trades many of their fathers work in; it will provide skilled labour in an area where there is a shortage; it will improve engagement, improve behaviour and give Kelsey kids who find themselves on such a course a huge and genuine advantage in the jobs market.

Where is the catch here? I see none. Like all truly brilliant ideas it is utterly simple, relatively easy to implement and the potential benefits are profound. Why doesn't every school in the country with a catchment who would benefit from such an idea have such a facility, so that kids who are turned off by their relative academic under-attainment by the age of 13 can re-engage, can gain a sense of pride in what it is they do during the day, can conceive of a bright future for themselves?

Perhaps because such a project has start-up costs, which in a short-termist world are felt to outweigh the vast long-term savings these projects would make in terms of dealing with the boys who might opt out at 13 and, consequently, grow up to be skill-free adult men with self-esteem issues and nothing into which they can pour their energies. Brian Lloyd's idea of what to do with Kelsey Park's Sports Hall is a good one. One that could go some way to resurrecting working class creative traditions, if it were rolled out across the country. It's a shame it is yet to receive funding.

White Working Class Language[21]

Topps', Bernards, Plymouths, Rockfords, Nuremburgs, Metrics, Belindas, Chalfonts, Four minutes, Sieg Heils, Emmas, Clements, Sigmunds: there are, count them, 14 separate phrases denoting haemorrhoids in my language. These include the seemingly impenetrable 'Judith Chalmers' (Chalmers – farmers – Farmer Giles – piles). The Eskimos? They have 57 different words for snow. In London, we too, are specialists ...

Our phrase 'gertcha', for instance (meaning 'Get out of it you saucy rascal. I believe not a word of it!'), can be used to exemplify the complex rules of my language. First of all, the 'g' is silent; consequently, its correct pronunciation, when given the appropriate guttural twang, is 'urrrtcha'. However, this pronunciation is itself altered when gertcha is followed by a word beginning in a consonant, the ubiquitous 'cowson' – meaning 'son of a cow' – for instance; in this case the final 'a' of gertcha assumes an 'oo' sound. Thus the chorus of the famous Hodges and Peacock song is pronounced 'Urrtchoo cowson. Urrtcha!'

There was a brilliant guy on *BBC London News* last year. From Lewisham, he'd overcome a previous overfondness for the lager and started making low budget feature films from his council flat. On his second or third film by the time anyone had taken any notice, he turned to the camera, and with the pluck, passion and bravery still evident in the best of us, emoted a line now etched in my memory, 'We are a

---

[21] This wasn't written for *The Guardian*. It was published in the *Teachit Newsletter* (for English teachers), and for some reason found its way onto the Standards Site (!) I felt it worth including here simply for the line, 'In London, we too, are specialists ...' which amuses me no end.

culture. It ain't no use just calling on us when you've got a war going on that you want us to fight for you. We want respect in peacetime too.'

And I, who still delights in going to the rub-a-dub with my old man for a sherbet and an oily (now sadly taken outside of the boozer), I wonder ... I wonder whether you, a teacher of language, a smart bird or a clever geezer in anybody's language, would think that I was thick for speaking the way I do; would let me know you thought I was thick; would correct me – publicly – for speaking the language of my heritage; would make me feel inferior; all the time telling my old mucker, Mohammed (whose sister I will marry one day), that his language is beautiful and rich and that he has a fundamental human right to it being seen positively – and all that!

If you have working class white kids in your class it is your moral responsibility never, ever, ever, ever, to even go so far as contemplating correcting how they speak. Their language is who they are. You 'aven't got the right to screw with it. How they speak is OK by you. How they write on the other hand: that's what you're paid to sort (out?).

White Working Class Boys[22]

It's bloody freezing at Sangley Road bus stop 6 a.m. The fancy coat I bought offers scant protection from the chill wind blowing in over Lower Sydenham from the Forest Hill slopes.

---

[22] I thought I would be recipient of a kicking for this one, and that *The Guardian* would cut it to buggery. They did cut it so heavily that much of the sense was lost. But the kicking did

There's not much company to be had on the early bus either. Me, a few morning cleaners and some men who, tough of spirit, work with their hands building some Docklands office block, which once built will nevermore allow them entry.

Every morning as I wait for the bus I see the same two old blokes. They are in their early 70s. Thin and white, they suck hard on wet roll-ups as if the ember of the cigarette would be enough to keep out the winter. Every morning they wait for the paper van. Every morning. To do a job that gives them more in the way of dignity than it does in money.

They are a strange species these ancestors of the near future; bordering on obsolete so the education system would have you believe. They are white working class males.

Forgive the dewy romanticism here, but these men operate as daily emblems in my life of something precious that I feel is ascribed insufficient value. White working class men, lest we forget, were the cannon fodder of two world wars, the group of people who adapted to live alongside immigrant communities and the owners of both a proud work ethic and a tradition of labour.

I wonder then why members of this ethnic and social grouping, the grandchildren or great grandchildren of the two old guys who get up at 5 a.m. each day simply so they may speak of their work, are so easily put aside by the education system?

The government White Paper in a section entitled 'Black and Minority Ethnic Children' quotes the awful and relatively

---

not materialise. Moreover, it seemed to ring a chord with many people who had been thinking similar things, but, it seems, were too scared of being the recipients of knee-jerk accusations of racism to raise their voices.

well-known fact that only 17 percent of Black Caribbean boys achieved the requisite standard in GCSEs last year. This is an issue that requires funding, input, new thinking and risk taking. It is also an issue that has had some publicity. People are aware of this crisis.

A four-line, tacked-on addendum in the same section reveals in a startlingly matter of fact piece of understatement, 'many white working class boys can also fail to fulfil their potential'. You can almost hear the subtext screaming, 'but that's OK. No one gives too much of a toss about them, their community and pressure groups don't have much of a voice, and they'll all get jobs as plumbers anyway.'

As the White Paper states, white working class boys who are eligible for school meals perform lower than almost any other group. Why then is the government's response to this catastrophe quite so glib. 'Some schools,' the White Paper says, 'have developed successful approaches to meeting the needs of this group and we will ensure that this best practice is shared more widely.'

I've attended one of these practice-sharing sessions. Last year, the Specialist Schools Trust invited delegates to learn from lead practitioners in certain key specialisms. It was a brilliantly run day, with several erudite speakers at the front end. My excitement, however, was reserved for one particular seminar, run by Robert Clack School in Dagenham, entitled 'How to Raise the Achievement of White Working Class Boys'. I hopped along to this, pen in hand, ready to make fervid notes.

I was to be disappointed. Sadly, there was no magic bullet, and little a classroom teacher could apply. Robert Clack School was quite simply a very well run school in a predominantly white working class part of town.

Why then are white working class boys doing so badly? A former colleague, Kevin Ducker suggests it is because of the patrician nature of the English education system: set up by the ruling and middle classes for their own benefit.

'Working class people have an established and justifiable resentment for most things they consider to be middle class,' my colleague writes. 'The white, working class never really feel part of the education system simply because they are not represented in it. When a teacher arrives in school who looks, behaves and sounds like them, in my experience, they react positively.'

So is it just a question of having no identifiable role models? I doubt this. There are many (though probably not enough) working class teachers in our schools. Where I do have some sympathy with my former colleague is when he gets onto more explosive ground.

'They also have to contend with the inability of schools to promote positive white role models and the steady erosion of their culture. Winter celebrations replace Christmas holidays, McDonald's the pie and mash shops and many of the once banged-out local pubs have been closed down. Is it any wonder that the working class feel disaffected and transfer this disaffection onto their children who arrive at the school gate angry and socially marginalised?'

It's all too easy for those living outside of such communities to dismiss such views as a retrograde longing for empire, or worse. But I too have sat through whole rafts of assemblies about Nelson Mandela, Rosa Parks and Jessie Owens, where the only white person mentioned all term is Adolf Hitler. And I've watched the white kids squirm with guilt, embarrassment and shame, as they are force-fed a daily diet of the doctrine of their own obsolescence.

I've always felt it to be a vital part of the curriculum that we study the impact of empire: not just British, but Belgian and Portuguese too. The 'Poems from Other Cultures and Traditions' section in the *NEAB Anthology* gives teachers a brilliant opportunity to cover these issues, and to discuss race, dialect and cultural heritage in an open and safe environment. But I still have this lingering worry that when asked for a positive white working class male role model we grope in the direction of David Beckham (alleged adulterer, devotee of Mammon and noted intellectual), and are then lost.

There must be more identifiably working class white male writers in Britain than Simon Armitage. Surely, there's also the odd chemist or mathematician. It'd be nice if white kids got to know about them.

It might also be an area for one of the government's working parties. The achievement of white working class boys is not high enough on the agenda: the fact that they are mentioned as a mere sub-section, an afterthought in 'Black and Minority Ethnic Children' proves this.

This positioning suggests that the white working class is now viewed as a minority ethnic community. I won't bother arguing the statistics here, but if white working class males are an ethnic minority, then don't we have laws about discriminating against them?

Class in the Classroom

What's the most you've ever paid for a book? I'll bet not too many have stumped out more than the 50 quid it costs to purchase a copy of Gillian Evans's *Educational Failure and Working Class White Children in Britain*. Furthermore, I'll bet, had you done so, you wouldn't have left your copy in the boozer, having to skulk back to Amazon, spitting, to buy a replacement.

Evans took her fair share of abuse when the book was published for having had the temerity to raise this issue at the same time as admitting that she was middle class. Many of the letters, when boiled down to their essence, were pointless parables of the fact that the writers' grandfathers used to live in a cardboard box in the middle of the road and lick the road clean with their tongues. There were countless accusations of class tourism, not too many expressions of gratitude for pushing this issue further up the agenda.

The importance of the issue raised in Evans's book is the stuff of the remedial maths lesson: if the largest cultural group in the country is utterly disenfranchised by the education system, the effect on national averages is necessarily going to be catastrophic. My cat could've worked this out. The bottom line of Blairism is the national average, and the drag that white working class kids' results place on these averages should mean that, ideological concerns aside, engaging them should be the very highest priority of the government's highest priority.

Yet the only solution it seems many are able to form is a cry for the return of the grammar school system, which wrote off the majority of working class kids at the age of 11. Why, aside from building academies on estates and fiddling catchment areas so they are filled with middle class children from other areas, has there been so little action on this longest standing of national crises? Is it perhaps that anyone brave enough, as Evans has been, to point out that white working class kids need and deserve specifically targeted input, fears being tarred a racist? Perhaps. Is it that the school is a middle class institution and that many teachers simply do not understand the culture of the children they teach? Perhaps also.

Whatever the reason, there is no evidence to suggest that governments have the will to solve this. All the way back in 1990 Chris Woodhead, in prescient mood, flagged white working class disengagement as being catastrophic: 'The failure of white working class boys is one of the most disturbing problems we face within the whole education system.'

It seems, at long last, that there are rumblings towards action. Mr Woodhead's observations have finally filtered down to the operational wing of the institution he once led. (It only took 17 years. If only he were as stern with his own staff!) OFSTED are making specific checks on how schools cater for white working class boys.

These, the words of an OFSTED spokesperson, by way of explanation: 'Before section 5 inspections, inspectors analyse the school's self-evaluation form and performance data, and identify issues to be investigated during the inspection. The achievement of White British boys might be identified as such an issue if it varies significantly from that of other groups of pupils.' Also, 'In 2007/08, Ofsted plans to undertake an additional exercise to identify case studies of good practice in promoting the achievement of White working-class boys.'

This collection of case studies, in response to the statement of intent in last year's White Paper, can be taken either as evidence that the tectonic plates are finally cracking, or that the wheels of regulatory authorities run so slowly as to be near impotent. They will eventually result in a report, which you will probably not have time to read.

Last year, Richard Stainton, of the National Union of Teachers' education unit, asked me to present some training on this issue. After an initial session in which we broke down the issue into 15 specific barriers to achievement, the delegates went back to their schools and started to do something about it. And you know, when you ask a teacher to do something to remedy a large scale social issue, a strange thing happens. Instead of debating it for 50 years, eventually coming up with a list of reasons something can't be done, they just do it.

Launcelot Primary on the vast and predominantly white Downham Estate in Lewisham, for instance. The head teacher of this school, Chris Childs, understands the reality of working class kids who, as Evans suggests, 'encounter the formal, proper, posh atmosphere of the school as if it were a foreign country'.

He does so by paying explicit respect to working class culture, not loading the kids with middle class aspirations. There are displays in which the children identify their heroes as relations who are plasterers; role models are not in the form of film stars and semi-literate football players, but people from the local community who have remained true to working class traditions and values. And these people are invited into the school, so that these values – being close-knit and protective of each other; having a rich, historic culture; a strong work ethic combined with humour and irreverence – are maintained.

Chris explains Launcelot School's approach: 'We want to be able to help our pupils to break free of limitations, so that they feel they can take some part in bringing about change, and have higher and realistic aspirations for the future. These are class related and very real issues for this group which are rarely acknowledged by the "powers that be".'

It is in places like Launcelot School, and in teachers like Chris and his team, that the solution to this age-old issue lays. Not in the slow motion impotence of the wheels of state. The classless society is a myth, and it is the responsibility of individual teachers and schools to bring the subject of class back into the classroom and assembly; to inform kids of their exact place, so that those kids might get angry, might re-engage and, in doing so, do something about improving their own chances. It is only teachers who can bring about change here, because as the old adage goes, 'If you want something doing well, you do it yourself.'

References

Adams, Douglas. (1979) *The Hitchhiker's Guide to the Galaxy*. Pan Macmillan: London.

Assessment Reform Group. (1999) *Assessment for Learning: Beyond the Black Box*. Assessment Reform Group: London.

Bosche, Suzanne, Hansen, Andreas and Mackay, L. (1983) *Jenny Lives with Eric and Martin*. Gay Men's Press: London.

Buzan, Tony. (2002) *How to Mind Map*. Thorsons: London.

Chalk, Frank. (2010) *It's Your Time You're Wasting: A Teacher's Tales of Classroom Hell*. Monday Books: London.

Cohen, Brad. (2005) *Front of the Class: How Tourette Syndrome Made Me the Teacher I Never Had*. VanderWyk & Burnham: St Louis, MO.

Cowling, Keda and Cowling, Harry. (1993) *Toe by Toe: A Highly structured Multi-sensory Reading Manual for Teachers and Parents*. Toe by Toe Publishing: Shipley.

Crossley-Holland, Oenone. (2009) *Hands Up: A Year in the Life of an Inner City Teacher*. John Murray: London.

Davies, Nick. (2000) *The School Report: The Hidden Truth about Britain's Classrooms*. Vintage: London.

Evans, Gillian. *Educational Failure and Working Class White Children in Britain*. Palgrave Macmillan: London.

Gardner, Howard. (2005) *The Myth of Multiple Intelligences*. Institute of Education Viewpoint Series: London.

Gervais, Ricky and Steen, Rob. (2006) *Flanimals of the Deep*. Faber and Faber: London.

Gilbert, Ian. (2008) *The Little Book of Thunks*. Crown House Publishing: Carmarthen.

Handford, Martin. (2007) *Where's Wally?* Walker Books: London.

Hornby, Nick. (2005) *Fever Pitch*. Penguin: London.

Klein, Cynthia and Millar, Robin. (1990) *Unscrambling Spelling*. Hodder Education: London.

McCourt, Frank. (2006) *Teacher Man*. Harper Perennial: London.

Whitwham, Ian. (2009) *At the Chalkface: Great Moments in Education*. Hopscotch educational: London.

Wiliam, Dylan and Black, Paul. (2006) *Inside the Black Box: Raising Standards through Classroom Achievement*. NFER Nelson: London.

Wilson, Gary. (2006) *Breaking Through Barriers to Boys' Achievement*. Network Education: London.

Wilson, Gary. (2008) *Help Your Boys Succeed: The Essential Guide for Parents*. Network Education: London.

About the Author

Phil Beadle is an English teacher, a former United Kingdom Secondary Teacher of the Year in the National Teaching Awards, and a double Royal Television Society Award winning broadcaster for Channel 4's *The Unteachables* and *Can't Read Can't Write*. He writes a column called 'On Teaching' for *Education Guardian*. This is his fourth book. His first was serialised in *The Telegraph*, his second has been used by Liverpool and Manchester United football clubs. He has been on Richard and Judy twice!

www.philbeadle.com

twitter.com/PhilBeadle

YouTube link http://bit.ly/philbeadle

Also by Phil Beadle

How to Teach: *The ultimate (and ultimately irreverent) look at what you should be doing in your classroom if you want to be the best teacher you can possibly be* ISBN: 978-184590393-0

Could Do Better!: *Help Your Kid Shine At School* ISBN: 978-055215511-3

Dancing about Architecture: *A Little Book of Creativity* ISBN: 978-184590725-9